Dubai

9/2285088

Front cover: Burj Khalifa
Right: Shisha pipe

TOP 10 ATTRACTIONS

Burj Al Arab The 'seven-star' hotel is the city's architectural icon (page 69)

The Gold Souk
Pick up a glittering souvenir of Dubai in this world-famous shopping quarter (page 41)

Sheikh Zayed Road Its futuristic skyline is home to some of the world's tallest buildings (page 54)

Downtown Dubai A clutch of record-breaking attractions centred on the extraordinary Burj Khalifa, the world's tallest building (page 58)

Abras (water taxis) Enjoy an *abra* ride between the traditional souks on either side of Dubai Creek (page 38)

Mall time Test your credit limit to the max in Dubai's dazzling array of shopping malls (page 60)

Desert safari Head out into the desert for an exhilarating 4x4 ride across the dunes (page 125)

Madinat Jumeirah A fabulous re-creation of old Arabia, with souks, restaurants, cafés and canals (page 67)

Bastakiya Traditional wind-tower houses are the attraction in the city's restored historic quarter (page 35)

Sheikh Zayed Mosque This Abu Dhabi landmark is one of the world's largest and most opulent mosques (page 82)

A PERFECT DAY

9.00am **Gold and spices**

After breakfast in your hotel, head to the glittering Gold Souk in Deira, exploring the gold shops and adjacent Spice Souk, combined with perhaps a visit to the nearby Al Ahmadiya School and Heritage House.

1.00pm **Wind towers**

Head down to the atmospheric Bastakiya quarter, with its marvellous old wind-towered houses, and grab a bite to eat at the sociable Basta Arts Café or the beautiful XVA Café and Gallery.

12.00pm **Historical interlude**

Spend an hour exploring the excellent Dubai Museum – an essential point of reference for anyone interested in the city's past.

2.00pm **Into the new city**

Catch a cab or take the metro for the short journey south to the spectacular skyscrapers of Sheikh Zayed Road. Get out at the iconic Emirates Tower and walk down the strip, admiring the eclectic high-rise architecture en route.

11.00am **Along the Creek**

Hop on an *abra* for the five-minute ride across the Creek to Bur Dubai, and walk along the waterfront to Shindagha for views of Old Dubai. Retrace your steps back through the souk to emerge by the Juma Grand Mosque and Dubai Museum.

IN DUBAI

3.30pm **Up to the top**

Exit through the back of the Dubai Mall to reach the heart of the Downtown Dubai development, with the Dubai Fountain in front of you and the huge Burj Khalifa, the world's tallest building, to your right. Head into the Burj and ride a high-speed elevator up to the At The Top observation deck (you'll need to have booked this in advance) for sweeping views of the city.

7.00pm **Arabian night**

There is a vast range of superb places to eat all around the Madinat Jumeirah — the canal-side venues are particularly lively after dark and a great place to people-watch. After dinner, catch another cab for the short trip down to the One&Only Royal Mirage hotel and head for the gorgeous little Rooftop Bar, which often has a DJ later on.

2.30pm **Shopping**

From the bottom of Sheikh Zayed Road bear left down Financial Centre Road to reach the main entrance to Dubai Mall. Spend some time here browsing the shops, visiting the in-house aquarium or going for a spin on the ice rink.

4.30pm **Sail of the century**

Catch a cab and head down to the stunning Madinat Jumeirah complex, explore the Madinat's souk, canals and shops, and then enjoy the unforgettable views of the sail-shaped Burj al Arab next door over a sundowner at the Bahri Bar.

CONTENTS

Features

INTRODUCTION

Nowhere is quite like Dubai. In the space of barely four decades, the city has transformed itself from a modest Arabian trading town, which few outside the region had ever heard of, into one of the planet's most glamorous, futuristic and talked-about destinations, home to the world's tallest building, its biggest shopping mall, its largest man-made island and a host of other record-busting developments.

Dubai continues to divide opinion. Politically stable, commercially dynamic and tolerant of other cultures and religions, for some, it's one of the 21st-century's great urban experiments; an attempt to create a truly global city at the heart of one of the world's most turbulent regions. For others it's the ultimate symbol of Arabian bling, rampant over-consumption, economic and ecological disaster-in-waiting and plain bad taste on an epic scale, appealing only to footballers' wives, millionaire playboys and the like.

There's a whiff of truth in the latter accusation, of course, and if you want opulence and excess, they can be found in Dubai. However, even a superficial acquaintance quickly shows visitors that there is a lot more to Dubai than Western tabloid newspapers allow. Development has been rapid and sometimes reckless, but Dubai now boasts one of the world's great modernistic urban landscapes – a 21st-century Manhattan, complete with futuristic skylines and stunning skyscrapers, from the soaring Burj Khalifa and massed towers of Sheikh Zayed Road through to the magical Burj al Arab.

For pure indulgence and hedonism, too, the city can't be beaten, with its glamorous hotels, marvellous restaurants and bars and superb shopping. And there's plenty of traditional

An aerial view at dusk of the Sheikh Zayed Road

atmosphere too in the old city centre, from the teeming bazaars of Deira through to the wind-towered mansions of Bastakiya and Shindagha and the old-fashioned abras that continue to ferry passengers across the Creek, just as they have done for over two centuries.

Dubai past and present

Modern Dubai's go-for-it dynamism is nothing new, in fact, and the city has always boasted an entrepreneurial spirit and ability to seize whatever opportunities it has been presented with. As early as 1894, Sheikh Maktoum Bin Hasher al Maktoum was enticing merchants from Iran and India to settle in the city with the promise of zero taxation, establishing the basis of the modern city's cosmopolitan, business-friendly orientation. Old Dubai was a flourishing port long before oil was discovered in the emirate in 1966, at various times making a living out of

Palm Jumeirah, one of Dubai's extraordinary Palm Islands

a vibrant trade in pearls and gold (often smuggled), as well as other commercial activities, and serving as a major regional hub.

The development of modern Dubai was dramatically kick-started by the discovery of oil in the 1960s, although Dubai's oil reserves have only ever been relatively modest, and only amount to a fraction of those in the neighbouring Abu Dhabi emirate. Oil production peaked at 410,000 barrels a day in 1991 and has been in decline ever since, with oil revenues now accounting for only around four percent of the emirate's GDP.

However, oil revenues provided the money to construct a modern industrial infrastructure, supervised by the canny Sheikh Rashid, who laid the foundations for the city's current prosperity. Rashid's son, Sheikh Mohammed, the current ruler of Dubai, has further accelerated the pace of diversification, overseeing the construction of lavish tourist facilities alongside a string of business-friendly initiatives ranging from assorted free-trade and enterprise zones such as Jebel Ali Port, Dubai Internet and Media cities, and the Dubai International Financial Centre (DIFC), all of which are aimed at positioning Dubai as the tourist, business and financial capital of the Middle East. Major global players have relocated their regional offices to Dubai, pushing the number of nationalities resident in the city to almost 200 and the overall population to over two million (up from under 700,000 in 1995). Foreigners now outnumber native Emiratis by more than ten to one, giving the city its extraordinarily multicultural and cosmopolitan flavour.

Not surprisingly, there have been growing pains along the way. Exploitation and alleged human-rights abuses of low-paid workers brought from India and Pakistan to labour on the city's endless construction sites have proved a running sore on the city's image. Social tensions between the many different nationalities cohabiting within the city also continue to provoke friction, while the regular incarceration of visiting

Dubai's Gold Souk

Westerners on charges ranging from carrying drugs to kissing in public has generated endless critical column inches overseas. Serious environmental concerns associated with Dubai's breakneck development are another major problem, while the city's creaking infrastructure, with inadequate public transport and horrific traffic jams, hasn't helped either, although the recent opening of the superb new Dubai Metro has at least gone some way towards addressing the latter problem. Worst of all was the 2008 credit crunch, during which the city teetered dangerously on the edge of bankruptcy before being rescued by oil-rich Abu Dhabi. Since then, many of the city's more outrageous projects have been cancelled, or put on possibly permanent hold. Even so, the city is once again looking to the future with renewed, if cautious, optimism, and though the freewheeling days of just a few years back are now firmly in the past, there is no sign that Dubai is likely to disappear anytime soon.

Beaches and shopping

Modern Dubai's attempt to conquer the global tourist market is based on a wide range of attractions. For visitors wanting a weekend stopover with sun and sand en route between Asia and Europe, Dubai provides the perfect choice, although equally, you could spend weeks here, exploring the city's myriad attractions and other sights across the UAE. The weather, too, is a major draw. Dubai is blessed with 12 months of sunshine, and although summer temperatures can reach punishing extremes, from October to

May Dubai's deliciously Mediterranean climate offers the perfect respite for sun-starved Europeans and North Americans.

Sweeping beaches and some of the planet's most lavish and memorable hotels are a big draw, while the city's outstanding range of top-notch bars and restaurants – which have established Dubai as something of a global culinary hotspot – add to the appeal, as do the extensive shopping opportunities scattered about the city, centred on some of the world's largest and most spectacular malls, many of which rank as tourist attractions in their own right. The city's magnificent modern architecture is also guaranteed to dazzle – Dubai is, after all, now home to the world's tallest building, and boasts more and bigger skyscrapers per square mile than anywhere else on the planet, New York, Chicago, Hong Kong and Shanghai included. And then there are the old city's attractions: traditional buildings with their distinctive wind-towers and sandy courtyards, the bustling souks of Deira and Bur Dubai and the Creek itself, at the heart of the old city, which is still busy day and night with traditional wooden abras and trading dhows, offering a living link with the Dubai of a century past.

Emirati dress

UAE national dress is worn in the workplace, at home and when out and about. The men's white, floor-length robe is known as the *kandoora* or *dishdasha*. The cloth headdress, which can be white, or red-and-white check, is a *gutra* secured by a stiff black cord known as an *agal*, with which Emiratis' *bedu* ancestors hobbled their camels' legs. Increasingly among young men, baseball caps are replacing the *gutra* and *agal*. The most visible items of women's clothing are the floor-length black cloak, the *abaya* and the headscarf, called a *sheyla*. Older women may be seen wearing the stiff gold and lacquer face mask known as a *burqa*, though this is increasingly rare. Children are often dressed in Western-style clothes.

Burj Khalifa, the world's tallest building

Layout of the city

Dubai is the second largest of the seven emirates that comprise the United Arab Emirates (UAE). Located northeast of the federal capital, Abu Dhabi, on the southern shores of the Arabian Gulf, Dubai faces Iran and has an eastern land border with Oman. The emirate covers 3,885 sq km (1,500 sq miles) of flat coastal plain and rolling desert dunes, with barren mountains, the Hajar range, in the distant east around the Dubai enclave of Hatta.

The modern city is extremely linear, stretching for over 20km (12 miles) from the old city-centre districts of Bur Dubai and Deira, on either side of the Creek, down to Dubai Marina (or "New Dubai") in the south. The multi-lane Sheikh Zayed Road runs the length of the city, connecting all the various districts and continuing to Abu Dhabi.

Transport within the city has been revolutionized over the past few years following the opening of the Dubai Metro. Further Metro lines and plans for new tram systems within Downtown Dubai and Dubai Marina should further improve matters, although most residents continue to get around by car, and traffic jams are an established fact of city life, particularly when crossing the Creek during rush hour, and down Sheikh Zayed Road.

A BRIEF HISTORY

The location of what is now the United Arab Emirates (UAE), straddling trade routes between the ancient civilisations of southern Mesopotamia (present-day Iraq) and the Indus Valley, and later between Europe and the Eastern colonies, ensured that the region has welcomed, traded with and been influenced by foreign visitors for several millennia.

The area that today comprises the UAE and northern Oman has been known by various names throughout history. To the Sumerians of southern Mesopotamia it was Magan, famous for its copper in the 3rd millennium BC. To the Persians of the 1st millennium BC, ruled by the biblical king, Darius the Great (521–486BC), Magan was Maka, which they incorporated into their empire in the 6th century BC. The Roman-era Greek historian and geographer Strabo of Amaseia (c.64BC–AD21) referred to the coast as the 'promontory of the Macae in Arabia.' To the Persian Sassanids of the 3rd to the 7th century AD it was Mazun, the 27th land of their empire. From the 4th century AD to the Islamic conquest of the 7th century, a significant number of its Sassanid-era inhabitants were Christians. The early church knew the UAE coast as Bet Mazunaye, and established monasteries along it. One of these, on Sir Bani Yas island in the emirate of Abu Dhabi, has been excavated and preserved.

Oil wealth

Dubai's oil was formed during the Cretaceous period, around 144–66 million years ago. It gave Dubai its great wealth during the second half of the 20th century, but by 2008, oil accounted for only four percent of Dubai's Gross Domestic Product (GDP).

Early civilisation

Though there are several important archaeological sites within Dubai's city limits, much of what we know about the region's early history comes from finds made since the late 1950s at other UAE sites. The earliest evidence of human habitation is a dwelling in Dalma, Abu Dhabi, dating back 6,000 years. Subsequent discoveries of prehistoric painted pottery pieces in the northern emirates of Sharjah, Umm Al Qaiwain and Ras Al Khaimah suggest that some form of international trade existed between the inhabitants of the coastal villages and the pre-Sumerian Ubaid civilisation, which flourished in southern Mesopotamia from 5600 to 3900BC. Also in Umm Al Qaiwain, archaeological evidence suggests a pearl trade existed in the 5th millennium BC.

One of the most famous archaeological sites in the UAE is Umm an Nar (meaning 'Mother of Fire'), near Abu Dhabi, a 3rd-millennium BC Bronze Age settlement that has given its name to the period in UAE history between 2700 and 2000BC. Camel bones found here and dated to 2500–2200BC are thought to be the earliest evidence in the world for the domestication of this animal.

Sassanid- and Abbasid-era ruins at Jumeira archaeological site

A significant Umm an Nar-era site in Dubai is at Al Sufouh, between Jumeira and the Dubai Marina. In the early 1990s, a circular Umm an Nar-type tomb and settlement was excavated here by an Australian team of archaeologists.

Iron Age

During the Iron Age, between 1200 and 300BC, the population of the Emirates would have been the largest up to that point in its history. Numerous mud-brick villages of the period unearthed by archaeologists include Al Qusais in Dubai, which is probably the site of a resettled Bronze Age community.

During the Hellenistic era, from around 300BC to a century or so after the time of Christ, two of the most important cities were Mleiha, south of Dhaid in Sharjah emirate and Ad-Dour, near Umm Al Qaiwain, which is the largest pre-Islamic site on the Gulf coast. Finds at these locations include Greek pottery, wine-jar handles from Rhodes and Roman glass. Aramaic lettering on much of the coinage found at Mleiha and Ad-Dour, as well as on stone and bronze inscriptions, indicates that the language of Christ was the lingua franca of the region in the pre-Islamic era, spread initially by dominant empires such as the Sassanids, and becoming the principal liturgical language after the Christianisation of the region.

In the late Sassanid era, a pre-Islamic trading post – a stop on the trade route between Mesopotamia and Oman – was established in what is now the Jumeira district of Dubai. Excavations have revealed the foundations of a Sassanid governor's palace, houses built of beach rock (*farush*) covered with lime plaster, and a marketplace. The settlement was subsequently expanded by the Abbasids in the early Islamic era. As a hub for East–West trade, under first the Sassanids then the Abbasids, Jumeira would have seen luxuries such as copper, spices, frankincense, sandalwood and teak move west, probably by sea, and valuable cargoes of gold, silver and textiles heading in the other direction.

Islamic era to colonial period

Arabic replaced Aramaic after the region converted to Islam in AD632. The first of the Muslim Arab dynasties was the

Umayyad Caliphate, which ruled in Damascus from 661. In 749, the rival Abbasids seized power and began to exert their influence in the area, as evidenced by the early Islamic-era additions to the trading post in Jumeira, the architecture of which reflects the Abbasid style.

In the late Islamic era, thanks to the skills of Arabic navigators such as Ibn Majid, inhabitants of the region traded with East Africa, and as far as India and China, as revealed by discoveries of fine Chinese porcelain fragments at coastal sites.

The earliest certain reference to 'Dibei' was made in 1580 by the Venetian court jeweller Gasparo Balbi, who was drawn to the region by the quality of its pearls.

The village of Hatta dates back 3,000 years

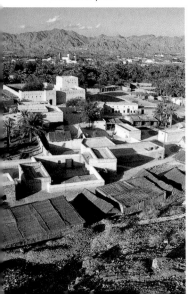

In the 19th century, the British asserted their control of the trade route to colonial India through a series of treaties with local rulers. One of these was Mohammed Bin Hazza, who ruled the small fishing and pearling village of Dubai from his Creekside Shindagha home at the time of an 1820 agreement. A British understanding with Hazza led to the first recognition on paper that Dubai was an entity separate from the more powerful communities of Abu Dhabi and Sharjah.

The Maktoum era

Dubai's modern history really begins in 1833, with the arrival of the Maktoum

family and around 800 of
their followers, who had left
their homes in Abu Dhabi
in disgust at the repressive
behaviour of the then ruler.
Installed in Dubai (where
their arrival instantly dou-

bled the local population), Sheikh Maktoum bin Buti took
over control of the town, inaugurating the Maktoum family dynasty, which survives to this day.

The position of the Maktoums was initially precarious,
wedged between the two far more powerful emirates of Abu
Dhabi and Sharjah, although the signing of a further treaty
with the British in 1835 afforded them some measure of security. Pearling continued to be the mainstay of the town's economy, while seaborne trade through Dubai also flourished, the
souk expanded, and in 1841 the new settlement of Deira was
established on the opposite side of the Creek. British influence
continued to grow, resulting in further treaties including, most
importantly, the 1892 Exclusive Agreement, whereby Dubai
agreed to hand over all its foreign policy affairs to Britain in
return for a guarantee of protection – an agreement which was
to remain in force until Independence in 1971.

Iranian influence

Another result of British influence was the arrival of the
first Indian merchants in the emirate – the beginnings of
what would later become a large community of Indian
settlers. The Indians were not the only foreigners to start
settling in Dubai. Of far more immediate importance was
the arrival of large numbers of Iranian traders during the
1890s. Increasingly punitive taxes in the flourishing Iranian
port of Lingah across the Gulf came to the attention of
Dubai ruler Sheikh Maktoum bin Hasher (who ruled from

1894 to 1906), who sent emissaries to Lingah to invite the unhappy merchants to Dubai, promising them free land and zero taxation. The Iranians arrived in their hundreds, providing a huge boost to the economy of the city (which soon afterwards overtook both Abu Dhabi and Sharjah in importance) and providing another cosmopolitan twist to the local population, as well as building the marvellous cluster of wind-towered houses, which can still be seen in Bastakiya. Dubai continues to enjoy close links with Iran to this day, much to the displeasure of the USA, and indeed of the federal government in Abu Dhabi.

The UAE's oldest mosque is at Badiyah, on the east coast

Sheikh Rashid

Dubai continued to flourish during the first decades of the 20th century, until it was struck by the crippling blow of the Great Depression in 1929, which virtually wiped out the demand for precious stones overseas. This devastated the local pearling economy, while the discovery of a reliable method of producing cultured pearls soon afterwards wiped out what was left of the industry, which had provided a livelihood for much of the population. Poverty became increasingly widespread, and the Deira side of the Creek revolted against Maktoum rule, leading to a state of virtual civil war within the city.

Fortunately, a man for the moment was at hand, in the form of the redoubtable Sheikh Rashid, one of Dubai's most visionary leaders. Rashid didn't officially become ruler until the death of his father Sheikh Saeed in 1958, but served as de facto leader for many years before his formal accession. His first major act was to crush the Deira rebellion in 1939, after which he had to face down a further wave of popular protests inspired by the democratic Arab Nationalist movement led by Egyptian president Gamal Nasser.

It wasn't until the end of the 1950s that Rashid was able to realise his vision for the city. His first act was to dredge the Creek, which had largely silted up, threatening to destroy the city's maritime trade. This he did, somehow raising the funds for what was then, in terms of Dubai's wealth, an enormously expensive project. Dredging finished by 1961, establishing Dubai as the best-equipped port in the region. (Sharjah, by contrast, allowed its own Creek to silt up during the same period and has been struggling economically to recover ever since.) Further projects followed in rapid succession: Dubai's first airport (which opened in 1960), the first bridge across the Creek (the Maktoum Bridge, erected in 1963) and, most importantly, the huge new Port Rashid (which opened in 1971), which did more than anything else to drive modern Dubai's nascent economy. At the same time, as if to prove that fortune favours the brave, oil was discovered. Reserves were relatively modest compared to those found in neighbouring Abu Dhabi, but the subsequent revenues provided much of the money needed to fund Dubai's major new infrastructure projects and launch it into the modern industrial world.

Independence

In the same year that Port Rashid opened, Du[   ] independent. The various "Trucial States", as they [   ] ously been known, had been living comfortably un[   ]

Life on Dubai's Creek before bridges transformed the area

protection since 1820 and had no particular wish to see the end of Britain's military presence in the Gulf. Forced to look elsewhere for protection, the emirates of Dubai, Abu Dhabi, Sharjah, Ajman, Fujairah and Umm al Qaiwain formed a new confederation known as the United Arab Emirates (a seventh emirate, Ras al Khaimah, joined soon afterwards), to be led by the ruler of Abu Dhabi, with the ruler of Dubai as his second-in-command. Many observers feared the new country would rapidly fall apart (or, alternatively, fall prey to a larger and more powerful neighbour), although 40 years later it is still going strong, and has proved more of a success than perhaps anyone could have hoped for at the time.

Dubai, meanwhile, continued to prosper within the new UAE. Business was booming, the population was growing steadily, and further landmarks appeared at the behest of the indefatigable Sheikh Rashid, including the new World Trade Centre, Jebel Ali Port, the Shindagha Tunnel and the city's dry docks.

Sheikh Mohammed

Sheikh Rashid suffered a stroke in 1982, and although he survived until 1990, the day-to-day running of the city increasingly fell to his four sons. Of these, the eldest, Sheikh Maktoum, was appointed official heir to the throne, although it was increasingly Rashid's third son, Mohammed, who provided the imagination and impetus that drove development. Mohammed continued to tread in his father's entrepreneurial footsteps, although focusing increasingly on service industries rather than infrastructure projects. His first major coup was the founding in 1985 of Emirates, now one of the world's most successful airlines. He also oversaw the creation of numerous free-trade zones and specialised business enclaves, most notably Dubai Media City and Dubai Internet City, backed with business-friendly legislation, which encouraged large numbers of blue-chip global companies to set up their regional headquarters here.

Realizing, too, that Dubai lacked global presence and an iconic landmark by which it could be recognized,

Naming rights

As Dubai teetered on the edge of bankruptcy in 2008, rumour abounded as to what price the rulers of Abu Dhabi would extract in return for bailing out their profligate neighbour – a handing over of Dubai's prized Emirates airline was one deal often mentioned, along with ownership of the Palm Islands or other choice pieces of local real estate. In the end, Dubai wasn't obliged to relinquish any of its commercial crown jewels in return for the loan, although it did make one small but richly symbolic concession, renaming the vast new Burj Dubai skyscraper as the Burj Khalifa in honour of Abu Dhabi's ruler Sheikh Khalifa bin Zayed Al Nahyan – meaning that the name of a rival ruler now adorns the loftiest and most visible building in the city.

Sheikh Mohammed decided to build one – the magical Burj al Arab, whose hugely distinctive sail-shaped outline has made the city familiar to millions. Further spectacular mega-developments followed, including the world's largest artificial island (Palm Jumeirah), its biggest shopping centre (Dubai Mall), its biggest fountain (Dubai Fountain), and, most strikingly, the world's tallest building, the monumental Burj Khalifa.

The credit crunch and after

Then, in 2008, just as it seemed the boom would never end, Dubai was brought crashing down to earth as the result of the global credit crunch. The real-estate market collapsed, investment fled, and Dubai, which had previously been announcing the launch of record-breaking new developments on an almost daily basis, found itself suddenly teetering on the edge of bankruptcy. Abu Dhabi eventually came to the rescue with a massive bail-out package, although many of the city's mega-projects were cancelled or put on indefinite hold, and now show little sign of being revived for a good few years at least.

The prime minister of the UAE voting in 2011

Overall, the credit crunch may have signalled the end of Dubai's rock 'n' roll years, although reports of the city's demise have been greatly exaggerated. With the aftermath of the Arab Spring still reverberating round the region, Dubai continues to weather the storm, and is facing the future with renewed, if somewhat chastened, optimism.

Historical Landmarks

2700–2000BC A Bronze Age settlement is established at Al Sufouh.

1st century BC An Iron Age village is established at Al Ghusais.

6th century AD The Sassanids set up a trading post in Jumeira.

AD632 The region converts to Islam. Arabic replaces Aramaic.

1580 Earliest surviving reference to 'Dibei' by Gasparo Balbi of Venice.

1793 A dependency of Abu Dhabi, Dubai is a fishing and pearling village of 1,200 people located around the Creek.

1833 Maktoum Bin Buti Al Maktoum and 800 members of the Al Bu Falasah section of the Bani Yas tribe settle in Shindagha, establishing the ruling Maktoum dynasty.

1853 The Perpetual Treaty of Maritime Truce is signed by Britain and local sheikhs. The region becomes the Trucial Coast.

1902 Increased customs duties in the Persian port of Lingah prompt more foreign traders to migrate to Dubai's free-trade zone.

1912 Sheikh Saeed Bin Maktoum becomes ruler.

1950s Electricity (1952) and a police force (1956) are introduced.

1958 Sheikh Rashid Bin Saeed, 'the Father of Dubai', becomes ruler.

1966 Oil is discovered in Dubai's offshore Fatah field.

1969 Oil production begins.

1971 The UAE becomes an independent federation on 2 December. Abu Dhabi's Sheikh Zayed Bin Sultan Al Nahyan becomes president, Sheikh Rashid of Dubai is appointed vice-president.

1980s First mall (Al Ghurair Centre, 1981), Dubai Duty Free (1983), Emirates airline (1985) and Jebel Ali Free Zone (1985) established.

1990 Sheikh Maktoum Bin Rashid becomes ruler.

2005 Population of Dubai reaches 1.5 million, up from 59,000 in 1967.

2006 Sheikh Maktoum dies. Sheikh Mohammed becomes ruler of Dubai.

2008 The credit crunch hits Dubai, pushing the emirate to the brink of bankruptcy and stalling many major construction projects.

2010 Opening of the Burj Khalifa, the world's tallest building.

2012 The Middle East's first ever female train driver starts work on the Dubai metro in January.

WHERE TO GO

Dubai – pronounced 'do buy', not 'dew buy' – is an extraordinary and surprising city. The cosmopolitan home to the vast majority of the Emirate's 2.2 million strong (and growing) population, its climate and beaches have met the two traditional holiday requirements of sun and sand for decades. Indeed, at one time sun and sand were about all the city could offer, apart from the Arabian souks on Dubai Creek,.

But in the last two decades, that has changed dramatically. The government's drive to uncover, preserve or rebuild heritage sites, which was initiated in the mid-1980s and gathered pace in the '90s, along with the development of a fascinating skyline with camera-pleasing landmarks such as Emirates Towers and the sail-shaped Burj Al Arab hotel, the development of world-class shopping malls and the promotion of the emirate's desert interior as a 'safari' destination for rough and ready exploration or luxury, reserve-based retreats means there are now so many places of interest that visitors can find themselves with little time for the beach – though world-class resorts such as Al Qasr in the Madinat Jumeirah and the One&Only Royal Mirage will surely lure them back to the turquoise waters of the Gulf eventually.

Within the lifetime of its oldest residents, Dubai has grown from three settlements of palm-frond, mud-brick and coral-stone dwellings based around the mouth of its 15km- (9 mile-) long creek – Shindagha, Bur Dubai and Deira, each little changed from the century before – to a modern metropolis that incorporates the once-distant fishing village of Jumeira and sprawls as far west as Jebel Ali Port, some 30km (19 miles) along the coast.

The Burj Khalifa dominates the city

Bur Dubai and Deira

Relations between the two Creekside districts of Bur Dubai and Deira have not always been harmonious. During the late 1930s, Deira rebelled against the authority of the Bur Dubai-based Sheikh Saeed, declaring independence. Order was only restored when Saeed's son, the young Sheikh Rashid, arrived in Deira with his Bedu retainers and shot down the rebel leaders. Those who survived were blinded in one eye as punishment and only allowed to keep their remaining eye on payment of a sizeable sum.

In the 1990s, the growth corridor was along Sheikh Zayed Road, southwest of the creek. Today, this eight-lane highway to Abu Dhabi boasts a number of eye-catching skyscrapers, including the world's tallest building – the Burj Khalifa – and, further west, the spectacular massed highrises of the Dubai Marina development. More recently, Dubai has been expanding into the sea and the desert. The Palm Island projects off the coast southwest of the old city centre are steadily adding more residential neighbourhoods and resorts to the city, while inland, new themed residential communities such as the Arabian Ranches are springing up amidst the sands.

But even as Dubai undergoes dramatic expansion to gear up for the millions more foreign residents, business travellers and tourists it hopes to attract in the years ahead, Dubai Creek remains the established heart and soul of the city. Dubai began on the banks of the Creek, and for visitors there's no better place to begin than at the beginning.

SHINDAGHA

The historic **Shindagha** peninsula on the western bank of Dubai's tidal Creek has now been swallowed by Bur Dubai, but was once a distinct settlement, separated by an arm of the Creek, known as Ghubaiba, which flooded at high tide.

A curling promontory at the mouth of the Creek, Shindagha is the most likely site of the original fishing and pearling village, which would have consisted of simple palm-frond dwellings called *barasti* or *arish*, and perhaps a few mud-brick houses. The main residential area for Dubai's Arab population in the 1800s and early 1900s, Shindagha was the traditional seat of the community's leaders. It was here in 1823 that Mohammed Bin Hazza welcomed the Persia-based British Political Resident in the Gulf, Lieutenant J. McLeod. Through an interpreter, McLeod briefed Hazza on British intentions along the coast, including plans to place a representative agent in the then more established settlement of Sharjah, to the north.

It was here, too, that 800 members of the Al Bu Falasah sub-section of the Bani Yas tribe settled after seceding from Abu Dhabi in 1833. Led by Sheikh Maktoum Bin Buti and

Shindagha waterfront, on the western bank of the Creek

Arabian architecture at Sheikh
Saeed al Maktoum House

Sheikh Obaid Bin Saeed Bin
Rashid, the Bani Yas influx
transformed the politics
of a community that had
numbered around 1,200
people before their arrival.
Maktoum became its new
ruler, establishing the Al
Maktoum dynasty that rules
Dubai to this day.

Heritage museums

The Maktoum family's for-
mer home, built in 1896 for
Sheikh Maktoum Bin Hasher Al Maktoum but now named
after his successor Sheikh Saeed, who ruled the emirate
from 1912 to 1958, was rebuilt in the 1980s and is a museum
of early life in Dubai. The imposing **Sheikh Saeed al
Maktoum House ❶** (Sat–Thur 8am–8.30pm, Fri 3–9.30pm;
charge) contains photographs, an exhibition about fishing
and pearling, coins, stamps and historic documents. Located
on a quiet stretch of the Creekside promenade, a 10-min-
ute walk from the bustle of the Bur Dubai *abra* (water taxi)
station, the two-storey structure, built of coral stone and
covered in lime and sand-coloured plaster, is a fine example of late-19th-century Emirati architecture, with Persian
influences. Architectural features include arched doorways,
sculpted window overhangs, vaulted high-beamed ceilings
and carved trellis screens, but the overriding feature of the
house is its four *barjeel*, or wind-towers, an innovative early
form of air conditioning introduced by traders from Iran.
The second-floor bedrooms and balconies above the high
perimeter walls offered vantage points for Sheikh Saeed,
grandfather of the present ruler, and his son Sheikh Rashid,

'the Father of Dubai', to watch the sea trade moving in and out of the Creek.

Today the view out to sea, across the busy road that leads to Shindagha Tunnel, is dominated by **Port Rashid**. Construction on this deep-water harbour began in 1967, instigated by Sheikh Rashid during an era of massive public works funded by the emirate's new oil revenues and designed to provide it with a diversified modern industrial and commercial base. The 3,300 sq m (35,522 sq ft) **Dubai Cruise Terminal** at Port Rashid makes the Shindagha peninsula a convenient first stop for cruise-ship passengers.

Pearl diving

Before 'black gold' there were pearls. In the centuries before oil was discovered, pearling was the mainstay of the Dubai economy, involving the majority of the Creek settlements' men and boys. From June to September, boats of between 15 and 60 men stayed at sea for up to four months, moving from one pearl oyster bed to another and sheltering from storms on Gulf islets. Equipped with little more than a nose clip, ear plugs and finger pads, and surviving on a diet of fish and rationed water, the men would dive on weighted ropes to depths of around 15m (49ft) up to 50 times a day. In two or three minutes under water they could collect up to a dozen pearl oysters.

Pearls were graded according to their size, colour and shape. In the early 20th century, the best pearls or *jiwan* (a derivative of 'Grade One' or 'G-One') could fetch 1,500 rupees, but while Dubai's pearl merchants grew wealthy, a diver's wages for the entire season could be as little as 30–60 rupees. Famous for their rose colouring, Dubai pearls were traded in India, from where they were sent to Paris. The popularity of the Japanese cultured pearl from the 1930s devastated the Gulf industry virtually overnight. After struggling on for another decade, the last great pearling expedition sailed from Dubai in 1949.

Peregrine falcons have a new role: hunting pigeons

Port Rashid aside, Shindagha, which consisted of 250 homes at the turn of the 20th century, was neglected in the rush to develop the city in the early years of the oil boom. When Sheikh Saeed died in 1958, the Maktoums moved away. But the regeneration of this stretch of the Creek, which followed the rebuilding of Sheikh Saeed's house, has seen the reconstruction of a string of other heritage houses. These include the Sheikh Juma al Maktoum House, an attractive traditional building from 1928, which now houses the interesting **Traditional Architecture Museum** (daily except Fri 7am–7pm; free), with informative displays on architecture and building in Dubai and the Emirates, and the nearby **Sheikh Obaid Bin Thani House,** dating from 1916.

A short walk north along the waterside lie the **Heritage and Diving villages** ❷ (Sun–Thur 8.30am–10.30pm, Fri & Sat 4.30–10.30pm). The **Heritage Village** serves as a focus for cultural activities, music and dance on public holidays and during the annual Dubai Shopping Festival in January (although the 'village' can be very quiet at other times), offering a glimpse of what life was like in the Emirates in the days before oil. On display within the compound are the camel- and goat-hair tents that nomadic *bedu* used before they settled on the coast, and houses of mud and stone that were typical of Dubai's mountain region around the inland enclave of Hatta. The nearby **Diving Village** presents a nautical variation on the heritage theme, with demonstrations and displays about pearl diving and the manufacture of fishing nets and traditional boats, which were made of palm fronds and wood.

Shindagha Promenade

One of the most attractive features of Shindagha, however, is the view from its promenade back along the creek, past the busy *abra* stations, the waterfront at Dubai Old Souk, the Juma Grand Mosque with its impressive 70-m- (231-ft-) high minaret and the Emiri Diwan (or Ruler's Court), towards architect Carlos Ott's sail-shaped National Bank of Dubai building and the triangular blue wedge that is the Dubai Chamber of Commerce. With the buildings crowded in on either side of the waterway, the *abras* packed with passengers criss-crossing

New millennium falcons

The fastest creature on the planet has been trained for hunting for thousands of years, but in the 21st century the ancient skill of falconry is maintained for sport rather than survival. Before weapons, peregrine falcons – which can achieve speeds of 320kph (200mph) in a dive – were used by *bedu* hunters to catch food. Wild falcons were caught and trained in two or three weeks at the start of the hunting season in October. Favoured prey was the houbara bustard, a desert bird the size of a heron, whose meat could be vital to a family's survival. At the end of the season, in March, the falcon would be freed.

Today, falcons are no longer captured, but reared from hatchlings. Even so, they require human contact on a daily basis, or else they become wild and unreliable. Especially keen falconers fly to Pakistan for hunting expeditions, their falcons travelling on their own special passports. Falcons are also put to practical use: Dubai's Burj Al Arab hotel employs a falconer to keep pigeons – and pigeon droppings – off the landmark property.

A water taxi on the Creek

the creek and the occasional passing *dhow* loaded with exports for Pakistan, India or East Africa, the scene is reminiscent of a Canaletto painting, recalling an old nickname for Dubai you don't often hear these days – 'Venice of the Middle East'.

BUR DUBAI

If Shindagha was the residential district of old Dubai, with no shops or souks, then **Bur Dubai** was its central business district. It was here that the first purpose-built office building, Bait Al Wakeel, was constructed in the early 1930s to house British agents and trade missions. Here, too, stood the headquarters of the British Bank of the Middle East, the city's first bank, established in 1946.

Historically more cosmopolitan than Shindagha, Bur Dubai was home to Persian and Indian merchants who settled here with their families from 1894, when Sheikh Maktoum Bin Hasher declared free-trade status for the city, though the major influx of immigrants came after 1902, when customs duties at Lingah, on the Persian coast, were increased and Bur Dubai became a more attractive hub for trade. The Persian influence on the architecture of Bur Dubai is still evident, in the 25 surviving wind-tower houses that make up the Bastakiya district.

Dubai Museum

The oldest surviving structure in Bur Dubai is **Al Fahidi Fort**, which was built between 1787 and 1799 to guard the landward approach to the town. The Portuguese-influenced fortress served as the ruler's residence and the seat of government in the past, and would have been a refuge for the inhabitants of the coastal community in the event of attack. The building itself – a simple, square, high-walled compound with corner towers covered in sun-baked plaster – is an arresting sight among the modern apartment blocks and office buildings of Al Fahidi Street. A stunning wooden pearling *dhow* stands on the plaza beside it.

Since 1971, the fort has housed the **Dubai Museum ❸** (Sat–Thur 8.30am–8.30pm, Fri 2.30–8.30pm; charge). Most of the excellent exhibits are displayed in underground galleries, including a multi-media overview of the development of Dubai, as well as detailed dioramas recreating scenes from everyday life in the years before oil. Among the artefacts displayed here are finds from the archaeological sites at Al Qusais and Jumeira, dating from the Iron Age and 6th century respectively.

Juma Grand Mosque

Between the fort and the Creek is the landmark **Juma Grand Mosque** (entry to Muslims only), one of the oldest in Dubai, which has the tallest minaret in the city, nine large domes, 45 small domes and space for 1,200 worshippers. It was built in 1900 and rebuilt in 1998.

Bastakiya

As recently as the mid-1990s **Bastakiya ❹** was a run-down place with up to 100 people crammed into a single house.

Traditional street stall in one of Bastakiya's narrow streets

Now, thanks to a restoration programme undertaken by Dubai Municipality's Historical Buildings Section, Bastakiya has become a case study for urban conservation in the Arab world and is enjoying a new lease of life as the city's arts quarter – particularly vibrant during the annual Bastakiya Art Fair (www.bastakiyaartfair.com) in March.

Located on the Creekside next to the Emiri Diwan, or Ruler's Palace, Bastakiya would not have been built were it not for the city's open-door policy to foreign trade. Its original residents were wealthy traders from Bastak and Lingah on the coast of modern-day Iran – hence the name. They settled here, close to their shops in the nearby Bur Dubai Souk, between 1902 and 1950, the period in which their distinctive wind-tower homes were built.

Bastakiya's famous wind-towers, which can rise to a height of 15m (49ft), were an early form of air conditioning – the open sides of each square tower caught the breeze and channelled it into rooms below. The walls of each house were made of coral stone, which, thanks to its porous nature, has low thermal conductivity, keeping temperatures inside to a minimum. For privacy and security, there were no windows on the ground floor, just a few ventilation holes, which gives the narrow alleyways between the brown, plaster-covered buildings an *Arabian Nights*-type atmosphere.

Wonderfully restored examples of Bastakiya's historic houses include the venerable **Majlis Gallery** (www.themajlisgallery.com; Sat–Thur 10am–6pm), which was founded by British expatriate Alison Collins in her family home in 1989; the **XVA Gallery** (www.xvagallery.com; Sat–Thur 11am–7pm), which has a calming courtyard coffee shop; and **Bastakiah Nights** (tel: 04 353 7772; daily noon–midnight), an Arabian–Iranian restaurant in one of Bastakiya's oldest and largest houses, built in three phases between 1890 and 1940.

Bastakiya is also home to **the Sheikh Mohammed Centre For Cultural Understanding** (tel: 04 353 6666, www.cultures.ae; Sun–Thur 9am–3pm, Sat 9am–1pm), which organises walking tours of the district, as well as guided tours of Jumeira Mosque and visits to local homes, to increase awareness and understanding between cultures. Public lectures on Dubai's heritage and culture are held from time to time in another house that has been restored and turned into a lecture hall, **Dar al Nadwa** (tel: 04 353 7373), which

The old merchant quarter of Bastakiya

Airline tower

The 55-storey 21st Century Tower is entirely leased by the Emirates airline, which uses it to accommodate its flight attendants.

was originally constructed in 1925 and restored in 2001. A stroll around Bastakiya will throw up other cultural curios, such as the **Arabic Calligraphy Museum** and a **Stamp Museum**, and photo-opportunities abound in its alleyways and plazas. Dubai Municipality's **Historical Buildings Section**, which is now based in a restored Bastakiya house, isn't a tourist attraction as such, but sightseers are welcome to step inside and view its courtyard and verandas.

Bur Dubai Souk

Known variously as the Abra Souk, Grand Souk Bur Dubai and the Textile Souk, **Bur Dubai Souk** ❺ (most shops open Sat–Thur 10am–1pm and 4–10pm, Fri 4–10pm) runs parallel to the creek below Al Fahidi Fort. Among its textile shops and stalls is a forerunner of the gleaming skyscrapers on Sheikh Zayed Road – **Bait al Wakeel**, the city's first office building. Commissioned by Sheikh Saeed in 1930 and completed soon afterwards, it was previously known as the Gray Mackenzie Building after the British company based there, licensed shipping agents in Dubai since 1891. Restored in 1995, Bait Al Wakeel is now a pleasant waterfront restaurant.

Nearby, at the water's edge, **Bur Dubai Old Souk Abra Station** is a fascinating spot to stand and watch the traffic on the Creek. For one dirham you can catch an *abra* (water taxi) from here to the Al Sabkha Abra Station on the Deira side of the Creek. From the water, you will get an excellent view of the traditional buildings on the Creek front. However, if you want to cross to the gold or spice souks in Deira, walk on to **Bur Dubai Abra Station**, near the entrance to Bur

Dubai Souk – the *abras* that depart from here will drop you closer to the souks. Air-conditioned waterbuses also operate from both stations.

For more contemporary shopping, **Al Fahidi Road** is lined with shop windows stacked high with shiny watches, mobile phones and other electronics, as well as colourful textile shops offering a wide variety of silks and fabrics from India. Further inland, Bur Dubai's main thoroughfare, **Khalid Bin al Waleed Road**, has the city's largest concentration of computer shops, while at its junction with Sheikh Khalifa Bin Zayed Road (Trade Centre Road) stands the expansive **BurJuman** (Sat–Wed 10am–10pm, Thur–Fri 10am–11pm), the largest and most upmarket mall in the old city and also the departure point for the amphibious **Wonder Bus** (tel: 04 359 5656, www.wonderbustours.net), one of Dubai's most unusual sightseeing vehicles.

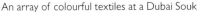

An array of colourful textiles at a Dubai Souk

Al Seef Road

Away from the heritage sights and the shops, **Al Seef Road**, at the Creek end of Sheikh Khalifa Bin Zayed Road, is popular with fishermen, walkers and joggers. Day or night, the view from the quayside in front of the British Embassy compound across the water to Carlos Ott's 125m (410ft) **National Bank of Dubai Building ❻** is one of the best in the city. In daylight, in particular, the bank's convex, sail-shaped glass facade reflects activity on the Creek below it, while towards dusk, when the sun hits the glass panels at just the right angle, the building shoots off dazzling rays of light. Next to it stands the triangular blue Dubai Chamber of Commerce. Water taxis and air-conditioned Waterbuses operate out of **Al Seef Abra Station**.

DEIRA

One of the three settlements that comprised early Dubai, Deira lies across the Creek from Shindagha and Bur Dubai. After settling in Shindagha in 1833, the Maktoums had to wait until 1841 before their power base extended to Deira. That same year, an outbreak of smallpox on the west side of the Creek prompted many of its inhabitants to cross to Deira and settle here. The early dwellings were made of palm fronds, but after fire ravaged the community in 1894, more substantial homes were constructed, using coral stone and gypsum.

A fabric salesman in Deira

Deira's great souk, Al Souk al Kabeer, was built in 1850. Stocked with imported goods, offloaded from *dhows* on the nearby Creek, it was the largest market in the region in the second half of the 19th century. By 1908, according to the historian and geographer G.G. Lorimer, there were 1,600 houses and 350 shops in Deira, compared to 200 houses and 50 shops in Bur Dubai.

Together with Bur Dubai, Deira formed the commercial heart of Dubai, but it was also the district where new services emerged: the children of Shindagha and Bur Dubai crossed to Deira for an education after the

Deira's Gold Souk has 700 shops

city's first school was established here in 1912, and people came to Deira for medical treatment after the first hospital on the Trucial Coast, Al Maktoum Hospital, was established here in 1949.

The Gold Souk

Arguably the most famous attraction in Deira today is the **Gold Souk** ❼ (most shops open Sat–Thur 10am–1pm and 4–10pm, Fri 4–10pm), a cluster of streets shaded by a high roof in the Al Ras neighbourhood.

The third largest centre in the world for gold bullion after London and Zurich, Dubai was trading in gold long before 'black gold' was discovered. In fact, when the bottom fell out of the local pearl market in the 1930s, after the development of the cultured pearl in Japan, it was gold that saw Dubai through one of its leanest periods. Historically, it was demand from India that drove trade, and even today, it is the softer, higher-carat golds favoured on the subcontinent that predominate in the souk's window displays.

With 700 shops, Dubai Gold Souk is claimed to be the biggest in the world, and with the lowest prices, too (haggling is expected), offering a huge range of intricately worked necklaces, bangles, rings, earrings and brooches in 14-, 18-, 22- and 24-carat gold.

A magnet for visitors throughout the year, the souk is particularly busy during the month-long Dubai Shopping Festival in January–February, when the area becomes a focal point for the raffle draws and street entertainment that are features of the festival. The biggest draw, however, are the discounts offered by traders throughout the month.

The Spice Souk

Closer to the Creek, at the intersection of Old Baladiya Street and the Creekside Bani Yas Road, is Dubai's **Spice Souk ❽** (most shops open Sat–Thur 10am–1pm and 4–8pm, Fri 4–8pm). Fronted by the restored heritage buildings of Deira Old Souk, just across the road from the Deira Old Souk Abra Station, the Spice Souk is smaller than it once was, but what it lacks in quantity it makes up for in atmosphere: the lanes here are much narrower and darker than the streets of the Gold Souk and the air is scented by the colourful offerings displayed outside each shop: cloves, cardamom, cinnamon, saffron, rose petals and incense. At an undefined point, the Spice Souk becomes **Deira Old Souk**, which offers an uninspiring selection of cheap cooking utensils.

Spices, nuts and seeds on sale at the Spice Souk

Al Ahmadiya School

There are several well-preserved historic sites in Deira close to the Gold Souk. Foremost among them is **Al Ahmadiya School** ❾ (Sat–Thur 8am–7.30pm, Fri 2.30–7.30pm; free), which is located on Al Ahmadiya Street in the Al Ras area, a short walk west of the Gold Souk. Al Ahmadiya School was the first semi-formal school in Dubai when it was established in 1912, and one of the Emirate's first regular schools when formal education was introduced in 1956.

Before it was founded by local pearl merchant Ahmad Bin Dalmouk, after whom it was named, boys were taught the Koran, Arabic calligraphy and arithmetic in their own homes by a man or woman known as *Al Muttawa* – literally 'volunteer'. With the establishment of semi-formal schools along the Trucial Coast, typically financed by pearl merchants, the curriculum expanded to include mathematics, sciences, history, literature and astronomy.

Al Ahmadiya School, Dubai's first, is now a museum
of education

Built in three phases, Al Ahmadiya School was initially
a single-storey structure with 11 classrooms and a *liwan*
(veranda), around an inner courtyard. The upper floor was
added in 1920. In 1932, following the collapse of the pearl
trade, and with it the local economy, the school was forced to
close, but it reopened in 1937 with a government subsidy. In
the 1950s, with the introduction of a formal education system,
English, sociology and more science subjects were added to
the curriculum and student numbers increased. By 1962, the
school had 823 students – more than it could comfortably
accommodate. In 1963, when it moved to a new, larger site,
the original building was closed.

During its restoration by Dubai Municipality's Historical
Buildings Section, authentic building materials such as
coral stone, gypsum and sandalwood were used to recreate Al Ahmadiya School as its famous old boys would have

known it. Among its illustrious alumni are Sheikh Rashid Bin Saeed Al Maktoum, ruler of Dubai between 1958 and 1990, and his third son Sheikh Mohammed Bin Rashid Al Maktoum, the current ruler of Dubai and UAE vice-president and prime minister. The school opened as a museum of education in 2000.

Heritage House

Next to Al Ahmadiya School is the similarly time-warped **Heritage House** (Sat–Thur 8am–7.30pm, Fri 2.30–7.30pm; free), which was also restored in the mid-1990s and opened to the public in 2000. The former residence of the Bin Dalmouk family, the pearl traders who established the school, the oldest part of Heritage House dates back to 1890, when it was built for Mohammed Bin Saeed Bin Muzaina. Sheikh Ahmad Bin Dalmouk expanded the house when he assumed ownership in 1910.

Today, the house is preserved as it would have been in the 1950s, offering an intriguing snapshot of the social life of Dubai's wealthier inhabitants during that period. Notable features include the separate men's and women's *majlis* (meeting rooms), where guests would sit on embroidered silk or wool pillows around the edge of a Persian-carpeted floor, drinking Arabian coffee and discussing the economic, social and political issues of the day.

Opposite Heritage House and Al Ahmadiya School, the small, single-storey building constructed in a similar style is Bin Lootah Mosque, built in 1910. Restored in 1995, the mosque is still used for prayers and is not open to the public.

East of the Gold Souk

Exiting the Gold Souk via the main entrance and heading east along Sikkat al Khail Road brings you immediately to the so-called **Perfume Souk,** comprising a line of shops

Old dhows lining Deira Creekside

along Sikkat al Khail and Al Soor streets which sell a mix of Western brands (not necessarily genuine) and more flowery local scents. Many places can also mix up a bespoke perfume for you from the rows of glass scent bottles lined up behind the counters.

Continue up Al Soor Street and cross the pedestrian footbridge over the main road to reach one of the most interesting markets in the city, Deira's **Fish, Meat and Vegetable Market** ❿ (7am–11pm), located between Al Khaleej Road and the Gulf. Although it is open throughout the day, the best time to visit is early in the morning when the market is busy with porters pushing wheelbarrows full of seafood between the refrigerated lorries and market halls. The variety of species is fascinating, some recognizable, some not, but including shark, barracuda, tuna, kingfish, sea bream, red snapper, hammour (Gulf cod), mackerel, sardines, squid and king prawns.

Returning to the Perfume Souk and continuing along Sikkat al Khail Road on your right, you'll see the narrow alleyways of the **Deira Covered Souk** which straggles all the way down into Al Sabkha neighbourhood, with hundreds of shoebox shops selling a fairly humdrum array of workaday household items.

Municipality Museum

The modern home of Dubai Municipality is on the Creekside next to the Radisson SAS Hotel, but its former headquarters has been preserved as another of Deira's heritage buildings. Located on the edge of the Spice Souk, across Bani Yas Road from the Deira Old Souk Abra Station, the **Municipality Museum** (Sat–Thur 7.30am– 3pm; free) is a simple but elegant two-storey structure with a long wooden balcony. Restored in 1999, the museum now hosts assorted civic documents and old photographs.

Deira Creekside

The Deira side of the Creek is much busier than the Bur Dubai waterfront, thanks to the *dhow* **wharves** ⓫ that line it between the Deira Old Souk and Al Sabkha abra stations. Although Dubai has two modern container ports at Port Rashid and Jebel Ali, as well as a busy international airport, traditional wooden dhows are still used for transporting varied cargoes between Dubai and its historic trading partners in India, Pakistan and East Africa.

The Municipality Museum

The activity on and around the *dhows*, which are sometimes moored three or four abreast, the tyres, automotive

Flying boat days

Dubai Creek was a landing area for Imperial Airways' flying boats in the late 1930s and 1940s.

spare parts and electrical goods stacked high on the quayside without fear of theft, the weather-beaten features of the old sailors and the timeless design of the vessels themselves make a wander along Deira's busy quays a highlight of any visit to Dubai.

Continue inland along the Creek for slightly over 1km to reach a second set of *dhow* wharves, occupying a purpose-built pair of quays between the triangular blue Dubai Chamber of Commerce Building and Maktoum Bridge. The quays jut into the creek here, offering an interesting perspective on Carlos Ott's **National Bank of Dubai** building.

Inland from the wharves, it's a short walk to the stylish **Hilton Dubai Creek** and, beyond, to one of Dubai's oldest landmarks, **Clocktower Roundabout**, where the Maktoum Bridge traffic intersects with Al Maktoum Road. Built in 1962, the venerable clocktower features in numerous old photographs. Originally surrounded by desert, it is one of the few structures to have survived five decades of development – a rare visual reference point in the changing face of the city. Overlooking Clocktower Roundabout, the identical towers of the **Marriott Executive Apartments Complex** are connected by a sky-bridge that, at 74m (242ft), is the longest in the world.

Not on the Creek, but just a short detour along Al Maktoum Road from Clocktower Roundabout, towards Dubai International Airport, is the **Nasser Bin Abdullatif al Serkal Building**, which is easily distinguished by its Indian-style architecture. The ground floor contains the nearest Dubai has to a motor museum: a display of historic vehicles (Sat–Wed 8am–1pm and 4–7.30pm, Thur 8am–2pm; free) collected by the prominent Al Serkal trading family. Among the vehicles on display are several Model T Fords, US military Willys Jeeps and post-war American classics such as the Ford V8 Deluxe, 1957 Buick Special and Chevrolet Fleetline.

Garhoud and beyond

Further down Baniyas Road you enter the suburb of **Garhoud**, close to the international airport, and boasting a mixed range of attractions. First up is **Deira City Centre** (Sun–Wed 10am–10pm, Thur–Sat 10am–midnight), one of Dubai's oldest mega-malls. It has long since been eclipsed by newer and more glamorous malls across the city, but continues to pull in a loyal crowd of locals, thanks to its wide selection of low-cost shopping outlets, which are busy at any time of the day or night.

Dubai Creek Yacht Club.

Past here stretch the beautifully manicured grounds of the **Dubai Creek Golf Club** (DCGC), home to the idyllic **Park Hyatt** hotel, the Dubai Yacht Club (where you'll find a number of lively restaurants, including the excellent The Boardwalk) and the landmark DCGC **clubhouse ⑫** with its distinctive tapering outline inspired by the shape of the traditional *dhow* sail, with three 'sails' entwined to create a tent-like structure – like a miniature Dubai remake of the Sydney Opera House.

The largest public park on the Deira side of the Creek, **Al Mamzar Beach Park** (8am–11pm; Wed women and children only; charge) is near Dubai's boundary with the neighbouring Emirate of Sharjah. The park, which is on a kilometre-long spit dividing the Gulf from three large lagoons, has four beaches, two swimming pools, lots of greenery, barbecue and picnic areas, children's play areas and an amphitheatre in which international children's productions are performed during the Dubai Shopping Festival.

UMM HURAIR

Moving away from the historic centre of Dubai, there's also plenty to see and do in the districts located to the south and west of Dubai Creek. Although they are referred to locally as 'the Bur Dubai side of the Creek', strictly speaking neighbourhoods such

Popular with families: leafy Creekside Park in Umm Hurair

as Umm Hurair and Karama are not actually in Bur Dubai.

Creekside Park

Umm Hurair's main attraction is **Creekside Park** ⑬ (8am–11pm; charge), which fronts Dubai Creek for over 3km (2 miles) between the

Arabian boats

The name given to wooden boats in the Arabian Gulf is *dhow*, from the Swahili word for boat, *dau*. These traditional cargo and fishing vessels are still a common sight on Dubai Creek.

Maktoum and Garhoud bridges. Together with Dubai Creek Golf and Yacht Club, on the opposite side of the waterway, the park is one of two green lungs in the centre of the city. Covering around 90 hectares (222 acres) and containing some 280 botanical species, Creekside Park is a verdant haven for rest and recreation and a focal point for activities during national holidays and festivals. It also offers fine views over to the Park Hyatt hotel and the quirky Dubai Creek Golf Club clubhouse on the opposite side of the water.

The park is also home to the vividly coloured buildings housing **Children's City** (Sat–Thur 9am–8pm, Fri 3–9pm; charge) near Gate 1, a fun, interactive learning zone and amusement facility for youngsters aged from two to 15. It houses several exhibits based around educational themes, including nature, space exploration, the human body, and local and international culture. There is also a planetarium and a special area for children under five, as well as daily educational workshops throughout the year.

Bordering the southeastern edge of Creekside Park is **Wonderland Theme and Water Park** (opening hours change throughout the year; tel: 04 324 1222/3222 to check; charge), a rather old-fashioned funfair and waterpark with around 40 indoor and outdoor rides, including rollercoasters and a log flume, as well as go-karting and paintballing. Its water park component is **Splashland**, which has several waterslides.

The impressive entrance to the Egyptian-themed Wafi Mall

Wafi

Not far from Creekside Park is the quirky **Wafi** Mall ⑭ (Sat–Wed 10am–10pm, Thur–Fri 10am–midnight), which looks like a little slice of Las Vegas dropped into the middle of the Gulf, with comic-book, Egyptian-themed design featuring a zany mishmash of huge pharaonic statues, hieroglyphs, spectacular stained-glass windows and half a dozen miniature pyramids dotted across the sprawling rooflines. It's kitsch but entertaining, while the complex also provides one of the city's most attractive shopping and eating destinations.

Beneath the Wafi complex is the beautiful **Khan Murjan Souk** (Sat–Wed 10am–10pm, Thur–Fri 10am–midnight), inspired by the legendary fourteenth-century Khan Murjan Souk in Baghdad and home to over a hundred shops retailing all manner of upmarket Arabian (plus some Indian) handicrafts. This is one of Dubai's finest exercises in Orientalist kitsch, with virtually every available surface covered in lavishly detailed Arabian-style design, featuring elaborate Moroccan-style tilework, intricately carved wooden doors and ceilings, and huge hanging lamps.

Next door to Wafi – and continuing the Egyptian theme – the vast postmodern pyramid of the **Raffles Hotel** provides the area with its most dramatic landmark, visible for miles around and particularly impressive after dusk, when the glass-walled summit of the pyramid is lit up from within, glowing magically in the darkness. Inside, the main foyer is well worth a look, with huge Egyptian-style columns covered in colourful hieroglyphs.

Karama

Some 2km (1 mile) away to the northwest, the low-rent suburb of **Karama** is one of the least exclusive and most popular shopping destinations in Dubai. A nondescript, and in places plain ugly, inner-city neighbourhood of 1970s low-rise apartment buildings packed with ground-floor shops and 'ethnic' eateries, Karama is Dubai's 'bargain basement', famous for its thriving trade in fake-designer gear and other cheap and cheerful stuff – you won't get more than a few paces into the main **Karama Souk** ⑮ before being regaled with offers of 'cheap copy watch', and the like. The quality of many of the fakes is surprisingly high, although prices can be unexpectedly steep – if you do decide to buy, check workmanship carefully and bargain like mad.

Immediately north of the souk lies **Karama Park**, a pleasant square of grass surrounded by dozens of inexpensive but generally excellent curry houses that have earned Karama the nickname 'curry corridor'. This is the social heart of the suburb, usually with half a dozen games of cricket in progress after dark, and crowds of strolling expat Indians, Pakistanis and Filipinos wandering beneath the trees.

SHEIKH ZAYED ROAD AND DOWNTOWN DUBAI

The greatest concentration of landmark buildings in Dubai is on **Sheikh Zayed Road**, between Trade Centre Roundabout and Interchange No. 1. From 1979 to the late 1990s, the most significant structure on this stretch of the highway was the white, 39-storey, 149-m-(489-ft-) high **Dubai World Trade Centre** building, at the northern end of the strip, which features on the country's Dhs100 banknote. Once the tallest building in the Middle East, it has long since been overtaken by much larger and more glamorous structures further down the road, although the adjacent exhibition halls at the **Dubai International Exhibition Centre** still see plenty of visitors during their regular programme of international trade shows and events.

The towering skyscrapers of Sheikh Zayed Road

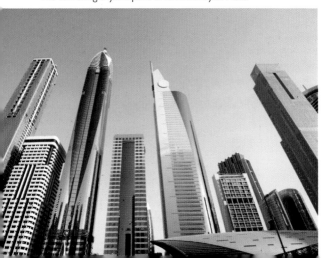

Just south of the Trade Centre rise the iconic **Emirates Towers** , completed in 2000, which consist of a 355-m- (1,163-ft-) high office tower – at one point the tallest building in the Middle East and Europe – and the 309-m- (1,014-ft-) high Jumeirah Emirates Towers Hotel. Visitors who aren't staying at Jumeirah (the 'h' on the end indicates a connection to

The Emirates Towers

the company that runs Jumeirah Resorts) Emirates Towers, or who have no business with the blue-chip companies based in the office tower should head there anyway, for a closer look at Hong Kong architect Hazel Wong's slender triangular towers, clad in silver aluminium with copper and silver reflective glass, described by Wong as 'a *pas de deux* in which the building facades capture the changing light of the desert sun and show off the dramatic integrated illumination at nightfall'. Inside the hotel there's a stunning 30-storey atrium with glass elevators whisking guests to one of the highest restaurants in the Middle East, **Vu's** (Sun–Fri 12.30–3pm and 7.30pm–midnight) on the 50th floor, or the separate **Vu's Bar** (daily 6pm–3am) on the 51st floor, both of which offer fabulous views of the coast.

In the ground floor of the complex, the **Emirates Towers Boulevard** is home to a small but exclusive collection of shops, with designer outlets including Cartier, Bulgari and Rivoli, alongside an excellent spread of restaurants and bars, including the ever-popular Noodle House (noon–midnight). Dubai's ruler Sheikh Mohammed and his entourage can occasionally be seen popping down here for lunch from their chambers at the summit of the office tower.

South along Sheikh Zayed Road

Immediately south of the Emirates Towers, behind the Sheikh Zayed Road high-rises, stretches Dubai's new financial district, the **Dubai International Financial Centre** (DIFC) ⑰. Entrance to the complex is via The Gate building, a striking office block designed in the shape of an enormous postmodern archway. Tucked away on the east side of the centre is the so-called **Gate Village**, home to a surprisingly wide (and non-financial) array of attractions, including some good bars, restaurants and shops along with a cluster of upmarket art galleries such as ArtSpace (Building 3), the Ayyam Gallery (Building 3) and a branch of the XVA Gallery (Building 7). Local office types flock to the village's watering holes after dark – popular venues include the funky Zuma Japanese restaurant (daily 12.30pm–3pm & 7pm–midnight) and the cool Gramercy jazz lounge (daily noon–midnight).

Café culture

Despite the futuristic architecture and roaring traffic, Sheikh Zayed Road is home to a surprisingly lively café scene, with many places tucked into the base of the soaring towers that line the strip. On the eastern (Emirates Towers) side of the road the chintzy Victoriana-inspired **Shakespeare and Co** (daily 7am–1am) in the Al Attar Business Tower, is a perennial favourite, as is hip **Cosmo** (daily 8.30am–1am) in The Tower, which has an international menu and shisha terrace, while there's more shisha at **Al Safadi** (daily 10am–1am) in Al Kawakeb Building A.

Places on the opposite, western side of the road include the fashionable **Olive House** (daily 9am–midnight), next to Starbucks in Tower No. 1, with good Lebanese cuisine, while the chic **Japengo Café** (daily 7.30am–12.30am) in the Oasis Tower offers an international menu with an Asianfusion twist.

The vast Dubai International Exhibition Centre

North and south of the Emirates Tower along Sheikh Zayed Road, the skyscrapers are lined up shoulder to shoulder, offering an eclectic compendium of architectural styles ranging from the elegantly postmodern to the downright weird. Notable landmarks along the way include (on the Emirates Towers side of the road) the **Fairmont** hotel, inspired by the shape of a wind-tower and strikingly illuminated in changing colours after dark; **The Tower**, covered in blue glass with Islamic styling and a distinctive pointed tip; the pencil-thin **Rose Rayhaan** hotel, at 333m (108ft) the world's tallest hotel; and the iconic **Dusit Thani** hotel, whose distinctive outline – like an upside-down tuning fork – is said to resemble the traditional Thai greeting of two hands pressed together. On the opposite side of the highway is the imposing edifice of the Art Deco-influenced **Shangri-La Hotel**; and the blue-and-white **Chelsea Tower**, with its distinctive square opening on the top bisected by an enormous vertical needle.

The Burj Khalifa

Just west of Interchange No. 1, the massive **Downtown Dubai** development was opened in 2010 and built at an estimated cost of a cool $20 billion. Rising like an enormous needle out of the heart of the development is the staggering **Burj Khalifa** ⑱, the world's tallest building. Opened in early 2010, the tower, at 828m (2,716ft), obliterated all previous records for the world's tallest man-made structure, smashing the previous record for the world's tallest building (formerly held by Taipei 101 in Taiwan, at 509m, 1,670ft) by a staggering 300m (984ft). The tower has also accumulated a host of other superlatives en route, including the building with the most floors (160), the world's highest and fastest eleva-

Burj Khalifa

tors, plus the world's highest mosque (158th floor) and highest swimming pool (76th floor). Much of the tower is occupied by private apartments, while 15 of the lower floors are home to the world's first Armani hotel (www.armanihotels.com).

The astonishing size of the Burj Khalifa and its distinctively tapering outline is hard to grasp close up – the whole thing is best appreciated from a distance, from where you can properly appreciate the tower's jaw-dropping size, and the degree to which it dwarfs the surrounding high-rises, many of which are considerable structures in their own right. The simple but elegant design (by Adrian Smith of the Chicago architectural firm Skidmore, Owings and Merrill) is based on an unusual Y-shaped ground plan, with the three projecting wings being gradually stepped back as the tower rises, so that the entire building becomes progressively narrower as it gains height.

The easiest way to visit the tower is to take the expensive trip up to the misleadingly named "At the Top" observation deck (on floor 124, although there are actually 160 floors). Tours leave from the ticket counter in the lower-ground floor of the Dubai Mall. Tickets cost 100Dhs if pre-booked online at www.burjkhalifa.ae or pre-purchased at the ticket counter. If you want to go up without a prior reservation, you'll have to fork out a hefty 400Dhs. Make sure you book well in advance – there's usually a waiting list of at least a week to go up the tower.

Around downtown Dubai

Immediately below the Burj Khalifa lies the spectacular **Dubai Fountain** ⑲. Standing in the shadow of the world's tallest building, this is, appropriately enough, the world's largest fountain: 275m (900ft) long, illuminated with over 6,000 lights and with water-canons capable of shooting jets of water up to 150m (490ft) high. The fountain springs into action after dark, shooting choreographed jets of water into the air which 'dance' in time to a range of Arabic, Hindi and classical songs, while multicoloured lights play to-and-fro across the watery plumes. 'Performances' are staged every 20 minutes between 6pm and 10pm in the evening (until

View of Dubai Fountain
from Burj Khalifa

11pm Thurs–Sat) and can be watched for free from anywhere around the lake.

Immediately beyond the fountain and lake lies yet another record-breaker, the gargantuan **Dubai Mall** ⓴ (Sun–Wed 10am–10pm, Thurs–Sat until midnight), covering a total area of 12 million sq ft (1 million sq metres), with over 1200 shops spread across four floors, making it easily the world's largest mall measured by total area (although other malls contain more retail space). Flagship outlets include branches of the famous Galleries Lafayette and Bloomingdales department stores, a huge branch of the Japanese bookseller Kinokuniya and an offshoot of London's famous Hamley's toy store. There's also a vast selection of upmarket designer stores, mainly concentrated along 'Fashion Avenue', complete with its own catwalk and Armani café, and a pretty Gold Souk with attractive Arabian design.

The mall is also home to the **Dubai Aquarium and Underwater Zoo** (Sun–Wed 10am–10pm, Thurs–Sat 10am–midnight; charge). The aquarium's most notable feature is the spectacular 'viewing panel', towering over the shops by the main entrance to the mall: a huge, floor-to-ceiling transparent acrylic panel filled with an extraordinary array of marine life, ranging from sand-tiger sharks and stingrays to colourful shoals of tiny tropical fish. All this can be seen for free from the mall; inside, the Underwater Zoo is more likely to appeal to children than adults, with displays themed after various different types of marine habitat and featuring an array of wildlife ranging from tiny cichlids and poison-dart frogs through to otters, penguins and seals.

Shops apart, the mall also boasts a host of other leisure attractions. Children will enjoy the state-of-the-art SEGA Republic theme park and KidZania, while there's also an Olympic-size ice rink.

Heading back to the lake at the back of the mall, a small footbridge leads across to the chintzy 'Old Town' development: a large swathe of low-rise, sand-coloured buildings with traditional Moorish styling. On the far side of the footbridge lies the cute little **Souk al Bahar** ('Souk of the Sailor'; Sat–Thurs 10am–10pm, Fri 2–10pm), a small, Arabian-themed mall specializing in traditional handicrafts and independent fashion. Restaurants line the waterfront terrace outside, offering peerless views of Burj Khalifa and Dubai Fountain after dark.

The Mall of the Emirates contains 400 shops – and a ski slope

On the far side of the Souk al Bahar stands **The Palace** hotel, its sumptuous Moorish-style facade and richly decorated interior offering a surreal contrast to the futuristic needle of the Burj Khalifa rising directly behind.

South towards the Marina

If you fancy a respite from the high-rise architecture, the lush **Safa Park** (daily 8am–11pm; Tue women only; charge) near Interchange No. 2 on the Arabian Gulf side of Sheikh Zayed Road, offers plenty of grass and fresh air and is a popular venue for walkers and joggers.

Alternatively, continuing south down Sheikh Zayed Road, it is a further 10km (6 miles) to the landmark **Mall of the Emirates ㉑**. Formerly the largest in the city, until being eclipsed by the Dubai Mall, the Mall of the Emirates is still one of the best places to shop in the city – and is less exhaustingly huge than the Dubai Mall. Mall of the Emirates has almost 500 shops, covering pretty much every retail option.

Shopping apart, the Mall of the Emirates is best known as the home of **Ski Dubai** (Sun–Wed 10am–11pm, Thur 10am–midnight, Fri 9am–midnight, Sat 9am–11pm; charge), the first indoor ski resort in the Middle East, complete with regular falls of artificial snow. This is the world's largest indoor snow park, with an alpine ski slope offering five runs of varying levels of difficulty – a truly surreal experience in the middle of the desert, and a great place to cool off when the mercury is touching 48°C (118°F) outside.

A short drive east of the Mall of the Emirates, on the desert side of the highway near Interchange No. 4, the functional **Gold and Diamond Park** lacks the atmosphere of the city's traditional souks but offers some of the cheapest gold and precious stones in the city – diamonds are a particularly good buy.

JUMEIRA

Running parallel to Sheikh Zayed Road, Dubai's beach-fringed coastline begins just west of the old city centre, running to the border at the port and free-trade zone at Jebel Ali, some 32km (20 miles) distant. The easternmost stretch of beach can be found in the upmarket but low-key suburb of **Jumeira** (you will also see Jumeirah with an 'h', which refers to the connection with Jumeirah Resorts). The closest coastal suburb to the old city centre, this sleepy area was where many expatriates settled in the 1960s, '70s and '80s and the suburb remains popular with wealthy expat businessmen and their wives – caricatured in urban legend as 'Jumeira Janes', who spend their days tanning by the pool of a private club and lunching with friends.

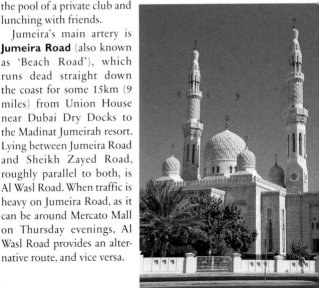

Jumeira Mosque, one of Dubai's most photographed sights

Jumeira's main artery is **Jumeira Road** (also known as 'Beach Road'), which runs dead straight down the coast for some 15km (9 miles) from Union House near Dubai Dry Docks to the Madinat Jumeirah resort. Lying between Jumeira Road and Sheikh Zayed Road, roughly parallel to both, is Al Wasl Road. When traffic is heavy on Jumeira Road, as it can be around Mercato Mall on Thursday evenings, Al Wasl Road provides an alternative route, and vice versa.

Coastal growth

Dubai's natural coastline is 72km (45 miles) long, but land reclamation projects are extending it by an incredible 1,500km (932 miles), which is longer than the natural coastline of the entire UAE.

The major tourist sight in Jumeira is **Jumeira Mosque** ㉒, at the city end of Jumeira Road. Built in the medieval Fatimid-style between 1975 and 1978, Jumeira Mosque is the only one in the city that non-Muslims are permitted to enter: the Sheikh Mohammed Centre for Cultural Understanding (tel: 04 353 6666) arranges tours on Saturdays, Sundays, Tuesdays and Thursdays, starting at 10am. Tours begin with entertaining and informative talks by a local Emirati guide on traditional religious practices, after which the floor is thrown open to questions, offering visitors a chance to quiz the guide on any aspect of the local culture's way of life. There is no need to book, but you should be at the mosque 15 minutes before the tour starts and buy your ticket outside.

Nearby **Union House**, a modest, round, glass-walled structure, is where the ruling sheikhs of six Emirates declared the UAE an independent federation on 2 December 1971 (the seventh emirate, Ras Al Khaimah joined in 1972). It's a short walk from Jumeira Mosque towards Dubai Dry Docks – look for the giant flagpole with the UAE flag.

Along Jumeira Road

The area around Jumeira Mosque, with its myriad cafés and small malls, is one of Dubai's nearest equivalents to an urban village. Across the road from Jumeira Mosque, Palm Strip Mall has the original **Japengo Café** (offshoots of which can now be found across the Gulf), while just a short walk away on the mosque side of the road is the ever-popular **Lime Tree Café** (daily 7.30am–6pm), another Dubai original, and the city's archetypal expat hangout.

Continuing west along Jumeira Road, **Jumaira** (sic) **Centre Mall** is home to the original Magrudy's book shop which now has branches in malls citywide and the coffee shop **Gerard**, a Dubai institution that has survived the influx of American and European franchise cafés and is particularly popular with young Emiratis. The next mall along, **Jumaira** (sic)**Plaza**, has a **Dôme** café that's popular with locals and expats alike. Across the road, the more modern **Village Mall** is the best in the area, with a small but rewarding clutch of shops including S*uce, one of the city's best places for independent designer labels, and another of Dubai's popular **Shakespeare and Co** cafés, with chintzy décor and outdoor seating in winter.

Close by, **Jumeira Open Beach** (also known as "Russian Beach") next to Dubai Marine Beach Resort and Spa and behind The Village Mall offers one of Dubai's biggest swathes of free sand. Bathers should beware, however: while the waters may

View of Dubai Marina from the beach

Jumeirah Beach Park

look calm, Jumeira has notoriously strong rip tides that can drag even experienced swimmers out to sea. While swimming trunks and bikinis are acceptable on the beach, bathers should cover up for visits to the cafés and malls on nearby Jumeira Road.

Just over a kilometre further down the road is the decidedly old-style **Dubai Zoo** ㉓ (daily except Tues 10am–6pm; charge). Founded in 1967, the zoo is the oldest on the Arabian peninsula, and it's very much looking its age, with overcrowded pens housing a motley assortment of animals, almost all of which arrived at the zoo having been taken from smugglers apprehended by UAE customs officials, amongst them giraffes, tigers, lions, chimps and brown bears, as well as local species, including Arabian wolves and oryx.

Southern Jumeira

Further southwest along Jumeira Road is the somewhat cheerier, Italian-inspired **Mercato Mall** ㉔ (Sat–Thur

10am–10pm, Fri 2–10pm), whose faux Tuscan and Venetian architecture has made it a tourist attraction in its own right. Inside, the large central atrium, with its glass roof, old clock, coffee shop and escalators, resembles a 19th-century railway station.

A couple of kilometres further down the road, **Jumeira Beach Park** ㉕ (daily 8am–10.30pm; Mon women and children aged four or under only; charge) is far and away the nicest public beach in the city. Entrance costs just a few dirhams, giving you access to a fine stretch of white sand (manned by lifeguards) backed by attractive gardens plus assorted cafés, kids' play areas and barbecue stands.

A short inland hop from Jumeira Beach Park, a residential neighbourhood between Jumeira Road and Al Wasl Road is the unlikely location of one of the Arabian Gulf's most significant archaeological sites: the **Jumeira**

Brand new old

The Madinat Jumeirah resort on the Jumeira coast is a reimagining of what Dubai could have looked like in previous centuries if builders of those times had access to modern construction materials and techniques, not to mention larger budgets. It mixes the wind-tower houses of the Creekside Bastakiya heritage district with the modest former palace in Shindagha and the souks of old Dubai, and stretches them upwards and outwards.

Designer Thanu Boonyawatana likened his approach to that of a movie special-effects wizard who, with the aid of computer-generated imagery, is able to recreate ancient Greece or Rome for cinema audiences: "We thought, "What if in ancient UAE or ancient Oman they had the money we have now and the technology we have now? What would they have built?" We built what they might have built with the resources available to us."

Archaeological Site (Sun–Thur 9am–2.30pm; free), where the ruins of a port town dating back more than 1,000 years have been uncovered by archaeologists since 1969. The original settlement, strategically positioned on the ancient trade route between Mesopotamia and Oman, dates back to the pre-Islamic Sassanid era, which ended in the 7th century AD. The site was built upon and expanded by the Abbasids in the first two or three centuries of the Islamic era and is today one of the largest and most important early Islamic sites in the Gulf. Excavated ruins include the foundations of several houses, including the Sassanid-era governor's palace, market buildings, a large caravanserai in which travellers would meet and do business, and a small mosque, although unfortunately they're all extremely fragmentary, and unlikely to mean much unless you're a trained archaeologist.

Jumeira's other sight of historic interest is the more recent **Majlis Ghorfat Umm al Sheif** ㉖ (Sat–Thur 8.30am–8.30pm, Fri 2.30–8.30pm; charge), Sheikh Rashid's modest two-storey summer resort made of coral stone and gypsum. Built in 1955, when this part of the coast was far removed from the city on the creek, the *majlis* was used by Sheikh Rashid, father of the current ruler, as a meeting house before becoming a police station for a time in the 1960s. A small museum now, the grounds have an example of the traditional *falaj* system of irrigation and a *barasti* (palm frond) structure with a working wind-tower. It is located on Street 17, off Jumeira Road – look for the brown heritage-site signs between Jumeirah Beach Park and Burj al Arab.

UMM SUQEIM

The Majlis Ghorfat Umm Al Sheef marks the southern limits of Jumeira proper, after which you enter the adjacent suburb of

Umm Suqeim (although the entire area is usually referred to as Jumeira). Here you'll find three of Dubai's most famous modern landmarks: the wave-shaped Jumeirah Beach Hotel, the spectacular Madinat Jumeirah complex and the iconic Burj al Arab hotel.

Burj al Arab and around

Without a doubt, the jewel of the Dubai coast is the **Burj al Arab** hotel ㉗ (literally 'Tower of the Arabs'), the city's best-known landmark, which since its opening in December 1999 has gained the iconic status of a Big Ben or an Eiffel Tower.

The unmistakable Burj al Arab

The 321-m- (1,053-ft-) high structure, shaped like a sail to complement the 'wave' design of the nearby Jumeirah Beach Hotel, dominates the surrounding residential neighbourhood and can be seen from virtually any point on the Dubai coast. A seven-star hotel, built on its own man-made island and comprising 202 two-storey suites, each with its own butler, Burj al Arab restricts access to hotel guests or those who have booked a table at one of its restaurants. These include the fabulous Al Muntaha (literally 'The Highest'), 200m (656ft) above the Arabian Gulf, with breathtaking views of the coast.

Best viewed from the public beach to the north or from various vantage points around the Madinat Jumeirah complex, the most distinctive feature of 'the Burj' is the double-skinned, Teflon-coated, woven glass-fibre screen facade, which is white by day and illuminated by coloured lights at night. The space-age helicopter pad jutting out from the top floor like a mini *Starship Enterprise* was famously used as a practice driving range by Tiger Woods and as a tennis court by Roger Federer and Andre Agassi.

Below the towering Burj Al Arab, next to the Jumeirah Beach Hotel, is **Wild Wadi Water Park** (daily Sept–Oct, Mar–May 10am–7pm, Nov–Feb 11am–6pm, Jun–Aug 11am–8pm; charge), which has 30 rides and attractions, including the Jumeirah Sceirah, the tallest free-fall slide outside North America, and the Wipeout Flow Rider surf pool, where budding surfers can ride a continuously breaking 3-m- (10-ft-) high wave.

Madinat Jumeirah resort: 21st-century luxury in traditional style

For an alternative and completely free way of getting wet, head to **Umm Suqeim Public Beach**, on the city side of the Burj Al Arab hotel. The view of the world's tallest hotel from this stretch of beach is stunning, particularly at sunset.

A stone's throw south along the coast, the splendid **Madinat Jumeirah**  (literally 'Jumeirah City')

Hookahs at the Souk Madinat Jumeirah

resort takes its inspiration from the wind-tower houses of Bastakiya, but modern construction techniques allow for taller, more impressive structures, making the resort a fabulous reinterpretation of traditional Arabian architecture. A definite 'must see' for any visitor, Madinat Jumeirah has two luxury hotels – Mina A'Salam (literally 'Port of Peace') and Al Qasr ('The Palace'), both of which have jaw-droppingly beautiful interior décor and a number of licensed restaurants and bars in idyllic sea-view settings that are open to non-guests (see page 135). A network of canals, serviced by *abra* water taxis, links the hotels and Al Qasr's 29 wind-tower summer houses with the souk and various waterfront restaurants.

Madinat Jumeirah is also home to the delightful covered market, **Souk Madinat Jumeirah** (daily 10am–11pm), which despite its recent construction manages to convey an authentic atmosphere. As well as various antiques shops, clothing boutiques and handicraft stalls, the souk has a number of bars, licensed restaurants and cafés that spread onto picturesque terraces.

THE PALM JUMEIRAH AND DUBAI MARINA

South of Madinat Jumeirah in the suburb of Al Sufouh, a multi-lane highway branches off the coastal highway to head out to sea and the remarkable **Palm Jumeirah**. Visible from space, the Palm Jumeirah is one of three ambitious palm-tree shaped land-reclamation projects off the Dubai coast.

As its name implies, the island is designed in the form of a palm tree, with the main road running down the central 'trunk', a series of sixteen 'fronds' spreading out to either side, covered in luxury villas, and an outer breakwater lined with upmarket hotels. Unfortunately, you can only really appreciate the unique layout of the island from the air; from the ground, the whole thing looks like suburban clutter, while the architecture along the main trunk road is decidedly humdrum, at

Atlantis resort

least until you approach the far end of the island, and the grandiose Atlantis resort hoves into view ahead.

Atlantis

At the far end of the Palm, the vast **Atlantis** resort ㉙ rears into view above the seafront. The resort is an almost iden-tikit copy of its sister establishment, the Atlantis Paradise Island resort in the Bahamas, with the addition of the few discrete Islamic touches, and looks like some enormous Disney palace. Inside, the hotel is as unabashedly over-the-top as one would expect. Entering the main foyer, you are confronted by Dale Chihuly's extraordinary sculptural instal-lation in the lobby – a towering glass sculpture looking like a huge waterfall of deep-frozen noodles. Corridors stretch away in either direction, lined with fat gold columns and vast chandeliers, while a floor-to-ceiling viewing panel offers spectacular glimpses into the vast aquarium of the hotel's Lost Chambers.

Atlantis boasts a host of (expensive) in-house attractions. Inside the hotel itself, the kooky **Lost Chambers** (daily 10am–11pm; charge) purports to consist of the remains of the legendary city of Atlantis itself, featuring a sequence of underwater halls and tunnels, dotted with specially con-structed 'ruins'. This is Dubai at its most shamelessly kitsch, although you may enjoy the sheer absurdity of the idea, while the 65,000-odd resident fish, both large and small, swimming around the submerged faux-classical remains, are impressive.

In the grounds outside you'll find the resort's spectacu-lar **Aquaventure** waterpark, home to a pulse-quickening selection of water-coasters, speedslides and power-jets, plus the dramatic 'Ziggurat' and 'Leap of Faith' waterslide, which drops those brave enough to tackle it at stomach-churning speeds down into a plastic tunnel in the middle of a lagoon full of sharks. There are also various gentler activities for

The gleaming white towers of Dubai Marina

kids (including a children's play area), while visitors can also use the fine stretch of private beach next door. The adjacent **Dolphin Bay** offers the chance to swim with the hotel's troupe of resident bottlenose dolphins.

Dubai Marina

Past the turn-off to the Palm rise the massed buildings of the vast new Dubai Marina development (or 'New Dubai', as it's sometimes called). This entire district is effectively a brand new city-within-the-city: a swathe of densely packed skyscrapers, which have mushroomed out of the desert with magical rapidity over the past five years or so. Even by Dubai standards, the speed and scale of the development here takes the breath away, especially for those who remember this part of Dubai in its pre-2005 days, when the entire area was little more than untouched desert, bar a modest line of hotels fringing the coast.

These upmarket beachside hotels remain the Marina's principal tourist draw, lining the long expanse of fine white-sand beach on the western side of the area. The hotel strip begins at its eastern end with the Arabian-themed **One&Only Royal Mirage** ③⓪, one of the city's loveliest hotels, followed in rapid succession by the Meridien Mina Seyahi and Westin hotels.

Past here the main road drops over the sea inlet leading into Dubai Marina itself to reach **The Walk** ③①, an attractive pedestrianized promenade running along the back of the beach, dotted with dozens of cafés. and restaurants. The Marina itself is a man-made sea inlet, around 1.5km (1 mile) long, dotted with luxury yachts and expensive speedboats and hemmed in by a positive forest of skyscrapers. It's an impressive sight, although the haphazard layout of the entire area, with random high-rises crammed pell-mell into every available space, serves as a chastening memorial to the super-fuelled property boom of the mid-noughties, from which the city is still recovering.

Religious tolerance

According to the Sheikh Mohammed Centre for Cultural Understanding (see page 37), 'Cultural and religious diversity has made the Emirates probably the most open and tolerant country within the region. Dubai and the UAE in general are liberal in allowing foreigners to maintain their own religious practices and lifestyles.'

Although Emiratis are Muslims and the legal system that applies to locals and foreigners alike is based on Islamic *Sharia'h* law, the Dubai government allows people of other faiths to gather for worship, as long as they don't proselytise Muslims. A number of Christian churches have been established on land provided by the rulers on the Bur Dubai side of the Creek. As Friday is the local weekend, most churches have main services then – Sunday is a normal working day.

Ibn Battuta Mall

Some 4km (2.5 miles) south of the Marina lies the quirky **Ibn Battuta Mall** ㉜ (daily 10am–10pm, Wed–Fri until midnight), situated in something of a no-man's land at the far southern end of the city, close to the sprawling industrial works and container docks of the Jebel Ali Free Trade Zone. The mall is one of the city's most outlandish but engaging

Racing camels exercise year-round at Nad al Sheba

attractions, inspired by the travels of the famous Moroccan wanderer Ibn Battuta, with different sections themed after six of the many countries and regions he visited – Morocco, Andalucia, Tunisia, Persia, India and China – all designed with Dubai's characteristic mix of whimsy, extravagance and high kitsch.

AWAY FROM THE COAST

Ras al Khor Wildlife Sanctuary

Close to Nad Al Sheba, the tidal lagoon at the top of Dubai Creek is home to the UAE's largest bird sanctuary, **Ras al Khor Wildlife Sanctuary** ㉝ (hides accessible Sat–Thur 9am–4pm), which can host up to 15,000 birds on a single winter's day, including between 1,000 and 1,500 migrant greater flamingos, which have been a protected species here since 1985. Other species that can be seen from the purpose-built viewing hides on Route 66 and Ras al Khor Road (Route 44) include Socotra cormorants, cream-coloured coursers and crab plovers.

Meydan

Evidence of the seriousness with which Dubai takes its racing can be seen in the spectacular new **Meydan Racecourse** just south of Ras al Khor (see page 88). The racing season is held during the cooler winter months from November to March, culminating in the prestigious Dubai World Cup, the world's richest horse race, with prize money of a cool $10 million. Race-meets are also a major feature on the city's social calendar, attracting a lively crowd of Emiratis and expats, although no betting is allowed.

Dubailand

The vast new Dubailand development has become the major symbol of Dubai's over-reaching ambition – and current financial difficulties. Occupying a huge swathe of land on the southern side of the city, Dubailand was originally

Dubailand plans

slated (according to plans announced at its launch in 2003) to become the planet's largest and most spectacular tourist development, with an extraordinary mix of theme parks and sporting and leisure facilities, covering a staggering 280 sq km (108 sq miles) – twice the size of the Walt Disney World Resort in Florida. Unfortunately, despite all the publicity, work on the many parts of the development now appears to be permanently stalled, and whether any of Dubailand's more ambitious features ever succeed in seeing the light of day is anyone's guess.

Parts of the development are, however, up and running, including the **Dubai Autodrome**, a 5.39-km (3.3-mile) Formula One-standard motor-racing circuit which hosts rounds of the FIA GT Championship); and **Dubai Sports City** ㉟, complete with international cricket stadium and Ernie Els golf course.

Close by on Emirates Road is **Global Village** ㊱, a combination of funfair and international retail park, with numerous European, African and Asian nations represented by elaborate pavilions. A spin-off of the annual Dubai Shopping Festival in January, Global Village is open each evening from November to February. Immediately past here, the swanky Arabian Ranches property development is home to the **Dubai Polo and Equestrian Club**, which hosts international polo exhibition matches in the winter months, and the unusual desert course at the **Arabian Ranches Golf Club**.

DAY TRIPS

The desert

A trip into the **desert** is highly recommended for all visitors to Dubai. The dunes that begin on the outskirts of the city continue into Abu Dhabi Emirate and eventually merge with the fabled Rub Al Khali, or Empty Quarter, the largest sand desert in the world. But visitors needn't travel far from Dubai to experience towering dunes, and pretty much every tour agent in the city offers popular (if touristy) half-day 'desert safaris', featuring some dune-bashing (driving at speed over the sands) followed by a visit to a desert camp for various entertainments including belly-dancing, henna-painting, camel-riding and so on. Most companies head out to the dunes around 'Big Red', a mammoth mountain of sand along the road to Hatta.

Several companies also offer longer and more rewarding desert excursions. Popular destinations include the Dubai Desert Conservation Reserve, in which herds of rare Arabian oryx roam free; Fossil Rock, where the fossils of marine creatures can be found on a rocky outcrop, confirming that this area was once the ocean floor; and Hatta Pools, cool

Hatta Heritage Village, built around an ancient settlement

mountain springs in the foothills of the Hajar range near the UAE border with Oman.

Hatta

The Dubai enclave of **Hatta** ⓷⓸, on the highway 115km (71 miles) from the city, can be reached by car in around an hour. Hatta's appeal lies in the contrast of its oasis greenery and rugged mountain backdrop, but its main visitor attraction is undoubtedly **Hatta Heritage Village** (Sat–Thur 8.30am–8.30pm, Fri 2.30pm–8.30pm; free), which traces the history of the settlement from its formation some 3,000 years ago to the 19th century and has examples of 30 traditional structures, from a fortress built by Sheikh Maktoum Bin Hasher Al Maktoum in 1896 to small mountain dwellings that wouldn't look out of place on the islands off the Scottish coast. The defensive watchtowers on either side of the heritage village offer superb views of the museum and the modern town. No day trip to Hatta would be complete without a refreshing drink, or perhaps a meal, beside the pool at the **Hatta Fort Hotel**, a popular weekend destination among Dubai's expatriate community.

Sharjah

On the coast north of Dubai lies **Sharjah** ⓷⓼, once the most important town on the Trucial Coast, but now overshadowed by its more glamorous neighbour. Nevertheless, Sharjah has a number of attractions to justify the trip out from Dubai. In the centre of town, the Creekside **heritage area** is home to several small museums and the pretty little Al Arsa Souk, while just down the road lie the old city **fort**, the **Sharjah Art Gallery** and the outstanding new **Sharjah Museum of Islamic Civilization** (Sat–Thur 8am–8pm, Fri 4–8pm; charge). Slightly out from the centre, the landmark **Blue Souk** is home to a good selection of carpet and handicrafts shops, while the nearby aviation-themed **Al Mahatta Museum** (Sat–Thur 8am–8pm, Fri 4–8pm; charge) occupies the site of the former airport, established in 1932 to serve the pioneering Imperial Airways route between Croydon, England and Australia.

Al Ain

The attractive city of Al Ain – the UAE's largest inland settlement – offers a rewarding day trip from Dubai, an easy 90-minute journey by car or bus along the swift E66 highway. The greenest city in the UAE, Al Ain grew up around the string of seven oases that survive to this day; the largest, right in the heart of the city, makes for a beautifully peaceful and shaded walk along narrow lanes threading their way between endless lines of date palms. The city is also famous for its fine collection of traditional mudbrick forts, including the striking Al Jahili Fort and the rustic little Sultan Zayed Fort, which

Al-Ain Jahili Fort gateway

Beach resort in Fujairah

stands next to the Al Ain National Museum. Nearby, the lively Camel Souk is also worth a visit, as is the breezy summit of the craggy Jebel Hafeet mountain, rising to the south of the city.

The east coast

On the east coast of the UAE, between one and two hours' drive from Dubai, the highway from Masafi to Fujairah passes **Bithnah Fort**, which in its mountain oasis setting is reminiscent of the great forts of northern Oman. **Fujairah** also has an imposing fortress with a mountain backdrop. The fort, attacked by British forces in colonial times, is believed to be the oldest in the UAE, the main part dating back 500 years.

The UAE's oldest mosque, built around 1446, is on the coast 38km (24 miles) north of Fujairah at **Badiyah** (non-Muslims usually allowed in outside prayer times). A short drive further north is the gorgeous **Al Aqah Beach ㊴**, a popular weekend retreat for Dubai residents, with a trio of upmarket hotels, including the landmark **Le Meridien al Aqah Beach Resort**. The clear, warm waters around nearby **Snoopy Island** are particularly popular with scuba divers.

Abu Dhabi

A quick two-hour drive down the coast, the wealthy and rather sedate capital of the UAE, **Abu Dhabi ㊵** offers an interesting contrast to its upstart neighbour Dubai, as well as a good selection of attractive beaches, swanky hotels and a couple of the country's landmark attractions. The major sight here is the vast **Sheikh Zayed Mosque** (Sat–Thur 9am–9pm, Fri 4–9pm;

free), completed in 2007 and one of the largest and most lavishly decorated places of worship anywhere in the world. The similarly vast and opulent **Emirates Palace Hotel** is another major attraction – afternoon tea in the grand lobby café is particularly memorable.

In the centre of town, the sprawling old **Qasr al Hosn** Fort and adjacent **Cultural Foundation** are currently closed for renovations, although the nearby **Central Market** – a stunning, postmodern souk designed by Norman Foster – should have opened by the time you read this. Other interesting traditional attractions include the well-presented **Emirates Heritage Village** and the old-fashioned **Al Bateen Dhow Yard**. On the outskirts of town, **Yas Island** is the venue of the Abu Dhabi F1 Grand Prix and home to the thrills and spills of the **Ferrari World Theme Park**, as well as to a handful of swanky hotels, restaurants and bars.

Sheikh Zayed Grand Mosque

WHAT TO DO

Dubai boasts attractions for all tastes. You can watch international entertainers and sporting champions perform, shop till you drop in the souks or air-conditioned malls, play on championship golf courses, or even ski on indoor slopes.

ORGANISED TOURS

Desert safari. Most 4x4 tours depart in the morning or late afternoon. Later tours are usually combined with a dune dinner and entertainment (belly dancing and henna body painting) after sunset at the tour company's torch-lit *bedu*-style desert camp.

Dhow cruise. A traditional way of experiencing Dubai Creek is by dhow, usually during an evening dinner cruise (see page 105)– tours are easily arranged through your hotel or any local tour operator. A more cost-effective and flexible option is to negotiate with an *abra* (water taxi) operator for your own tour of the Creek, which costs Dhs100 per hour per boat (irrespective of the number of people on it).

Air tours. A number of tour operators offer helicopter tours – Aerogulf (04 220 0331, www.aerogulfservices.com) is one of the best established. Prices are around $200 for a 15-minute flight. For hot-air ballooning over the desert contact Balloon Adventures Dubai (tel: 04 285 4949, www.ballooning.ae).

SPORT

Participant sports

Desert sports. Novel sports include sand-skiing and sand-boarding, which visitors can try on organised tours.

Evening excursion to the Sahara

Golf. Dubai's most famous 18-hole courses are at the Emirates and Dubai Creek (both tel: 04 380 1234) clubs. The Emirates' 7,211-yard Majlis is the venue for the Dubai Desert Classic, but newer courses such as the Montgomerie at Emirates Hills (tel: 04 390 5600), designed by Colin Montgomerie, and the Desert Course at Arabian Ranches (tel: 04 366 3000), designed by Ian Baker-Finch with Nicklaus Design, are fast gaining international reputations. More recent additions include the course at the Al Badia Golf Club in Festival City (tel: 04 601 0101), designed by Robert Trent Jones II; the 'desert links' style course at the Els Club at Dubai Sports City in Dubailand (tel: 04 425 1010); and the Jumeirah Golf Estates in Dubai Marina (tel: 04 390 3333), which has four courses designed by Greg Norman, Vijay Singh, Sergio Garcia and Pete Dye, and is the current home of the Dubai World Championship.

Skiing. The Middle East's first indoor ski resort, Ski Dubai at Mall of the Emirates (Sun–Wed 10am–11pm, Thur 10am–midnight, Fri 9am–midnight, Sat 9am–11pm), has five ski runs of up to 400 metres on artificially produced snow, including the world's first indoor black run, and a Snow Park with a snowball-throwing gallery. The entry pass includes warm clothing, but not hats or gloves. Absolute beginners are not allowed on the slopes

Spa days

Spa treatments are big business in Dubai. Most of the bigger hotels have spas – many of them offering lavish treatments in idyllic surroundings – the Assawan spa at the Burj al Arab, Amara spa at the Park Hyatt Hotel, Spa and Oriental Hamman at the One&Only Royal Mirage and Talise spa at Madinat Jumeirah are four of the most memorable. There are also some independent, and more affordable places – Cleopatra's Spa in Wafi is one of the best, while some of the city's numerous nail bars (N Bar is the main chain) also offer assorted massages.

without first taking lessons at the Snow School.

Tennis. Most of Dubai's resort hotels have good-quality hard courts as part of their fitness-centre offerings. Dubai's premier tennis venue is The Aviation Club in Garhoud (tel: 04 282 4122). Courts are available to non-members on an hourly basis for a charge that includes use of the club's other facilities. There are public tennis courts in Safa Park (tel: 04 349 2111).

Watersports. The beach-front resort hotels are the easiest places to arrange watersports. All the marina beach hotels (apart from the Ritz-Carlton) have their own watersports centres, with

Dubai is home to the first indoor ski slope in the Middle East

activities including windsurfing, sailing, kayaking, water-skiing, wakeboarding and parasailing. Local operators include Sky & Sea Adventure (tel: 04 399 9005, www.watersportsdubai.com), who can be found at the Sheraton Jumeirah Beach and Hilton Jumeirah Resort. For offshore sailing try Bluesail Dubai (tel: 04 882 3129) or the Dubai Offshore Sailing Club (tel: 04 394 1669). The centre for sailing on the coast is Dubai International Marine Club (DIMC) in Mina Seyahi (tel: 04 399 5777).

Spectator sports

Golf. The Dubai Desert Classic (www.dubaidesertclassic. com) is a major tournament on the PGA European Tour, held annually in Feb/March at the Emirates Golf Club. The four-day tournament attracts the biggest names in the sport – former winners include Ernie Els, Tiger Woods and Colin Montgomerie.

Horse racing. The racing season at Meydan Racecourse (www.meydan.ae) runs between November and March, with afternoon and evening races (mainly on Thursdays, Friday and sometimes Saturdays) culminating in the richest race day in the world, the US$10 million Dubai World Cup (www.dubaiworldcup.com). See www.dubairacingclub.com or http://emiratesracing.com for details of forthcoming events.

Rugby. The Dubai Rugby Sevens (www.dubairugby7s.com), part of the IRB Sevens World Series, has grown to rival the Hong Kong Sevens in terms of the atmosphere around its

The racing Maktoums

Dubai's ruling family has become synonymous with international horse racing, thanks mostly to the success of the Godolphin stable, established by Sheikh Mohammed and his brother Sheikh Hamdan in 1994 and named after Godolphin Arabian, a horse that was taken from the Yemeni desert to Europe in the early 18th century to become one of the three founding stallions of the modern thoroughbred.

The stable has trained such greats as Lammtarra, Swain, Daylami and Dubai Millennium. Typically, after a winter in Dubai, the Godolphin team heads to Europe, where its horses are stabled for the summer in Newmarket, the English town where Sheikh Mohammed is said to have acquired his love for horse racing in the 1960s while studying in nearby Cambridge. From Newmarket, the horses travel the world, to be ridden by the world's top jockeys, competing in the stable's distinctive blue silks.

On top of their Godolphin interests, the Maktoums also have private studs. In 1997, the late Sheikh Maktoum was the most successful owner in Europe, with group wins in five countries.

22,000-seat main pitch. The three-day event is held in late November/early December at the purpose-built The Sevens stadium on Al Ain Road, past Dubailand.

Tennis. The two-week Dubai Tennis Championships (www. dubaitennischampionships. com), at the Aviation Club in late February/early March, consists of separate, back-to-back women's WTA and men's ATP tournaments and

The Dubai World Cup is horse racing's richest prize

attracts the world's top players. The annual ITF Al Habtoor Tennis Challenge, held at the Habtoor Grand Resort and Spa in Mina Seyahi, attracts the rising stars of the women's game.

Camel racing. The city's old camel racetrack at Nad al Sheba has now closed; the nearest camel-racing track is the Al Lisaili Race Track, some 40km (25 miles) from Dubai, off exit 37 of the Al Ain road. Races are held from September to May, usually early in the morning around 6/7am.

Motorsport. Dubai Autodrome hosts the annual Dubai 24 Hour (a kind of local Le Mans), but most of the action is in neighbouring Abu Dhabi, which hosts the annual Abu Dhabi F1 Grand Prix as well as the Abu Dhabi Desert Challenge (www.abudhabidesertchallenge.com), an FIA-sanctioned off-road motor rally that covers some 2,000km (1,200 miles) of the desert interior in early April.

Water sports. Sailing and rowing races for traditional boats are held off Mina Seyahi and on Dubai Creek several times a year. The Mina Seyahi coast also hosts two rounds of the UIM Class I World Powerboat Championship in November/December.

OUTDOOR PURSUITS

Desert safaris. See page 125

Horse riding. Dubai Polo and Equestrian Club (tel: 04 361 8111) at Arabian Ranches offers desert rides and lessons. Other venues include Emirates Equestrian Centre (tel: 04 558 7656), out in the desert not far from the Bab al Shams hotel.

Quad biking. For quad biking in the desert dunes, head for the cluster of small activity centres some 50km (31 miles) from the city, on Route 44 to Hatta.

Scuba diving. The Pavilion Dive Centre (tel: 04 406 8828) at the Jumeirah Beach Hotel offers a range of on-site PADI courses and introductory dives, plus dives to nearby wrecks and one- to three-day excursions to Musandam. Al Boom Diving (www.alboomdiving.com) operates dive centres at the Jebel Ali Golf Resort and Spa in the far south of the city, and at the Al Aqah Méridien hotel in Fujairah, offering a range of PADI courses and dives, plus Musandam excursions.

SHOPPING

With thriving souks, modern malls and the annual Dubai Shopping Festival (DSF), which starts in January, Dubai is the proverbial shopper's paradise.

Where to buy

Souks. Dubai's most famous souk is the Gold Souk in Deira. Nearby is the Spice Souk, where frankincense and saffron are on offer. Across the Creek, Bur Dubai Souk is the place for textiles. Generally, most shops open Sat–Thur 10am–1pm and 4–10pm, Fri 4–10pm. Bargaining is expected and shoppers should always ask for the 'best price'. The down-at-heel Karama Souk remains popular, thanks to its vast quantities of designer fakes, cheap clothes and souvenirs. For a modern remake of the traditional Arabian souk, head either to the lovely Souk Madinat Jumeirah or the opulent new Khan Murjan Souk, both of which boast lavish décor and an Arabian Nights atmosphere – although prices are high.

Malls. In a city where temperatures can reach uncomfortable highs, Dubai's ultra-modern malls offer comfortable air-conditioned shopping, often amidst spectacular surroundings. Opening hours are generally daily 10am–10pm, and until midnight on Thursday, Friday and Saturday, though some are closed on Friday mornings. Prices are fixed.

Inside the Mall of the Emirates

For pure retail excess, the supersized Dubai Mall has by far the biggest selection of shops, while there are also shops galore at other major malls such as the Mall of the Emirates on Sheikh Zayed Road in Al Barsha, Festival Centre in Festival City, Ibn Battuta Mall and Marina Mall in Dubai Marina, Wafi in Oud Metha, BurJuman in Bur Dubai, Deira City Centre in Garhoud and Mirdif City Centre in Mirdif. There are plenty of smaller malls too, including the exclusive Emirates Towers Boulevard and the chain of malls lining the northern end of Jumeira Road.

Dubai's malls get particularly busy during the annual Dubai Shopping Festival (January–February), when shops across the city offer discounts and promotions, backed up by a lively programme of mall-based prize draws and entertainments. Dubai Summer Surprises (June–July) is another shopping-centred festival, with a similar range of discounts and in-mall entertainment designed to lure in punters during the hot summer months.

What to buy

Gold. Deira's famous Gold Souk is the focus of Dubai's roaring gold trade, although there are plenty of dedicated gold shops nearby, opposite the Gold Souk bus station and in the southern city near Mall of the Emirates at the Gold and Diamond Park. Items are priced by weight according to the daily gold price, although bargaining is essential.

Be prepared to bargain at the Gold Souk

Carpets. The greatest concentration of carpet shops is in Deira Tower on Baniyas Square in Deira, while there are also carpet shops in most of the main malls (Emad Carpets and the Persian Carpet House are the main chains), although prices are significantly higher. The best buys are to be had at 'Carpet Oasis' during the annual shopping festival in January (check the local press for venue details). The Blue Souk in Sharjah also has some excellent carpet shops.

Fabrics. Thanks to its long-established links with India, Dubai is a great place for high-quality, low-cost fabrics. Bur Dubai Souk has a concentration of textile traders, while nearby Al Fahidi Street also has some very good shops. Pashminas are widely available.

Perfume. Distinctive Arabian scents are available from Ajmal Perfumes and Arabian Oud, which have branches

Dubai Shopping Festival

The month-long Dubai Shopping Festival (DSF) was established in 1996. As many as 3.2 million visitors attend this retail extravaganza, which usually starts in January.

in many of the city's major malls. Alternatively, head for the Perfume Souk in Deira. Many places (including Ajmal) offer the chance to mix your own bespoke scents.

Souvenirs. There are souvenir shops in pretty much all the main malls in Dubai. For traditional Arabian artefacts (coffeepots, *shisha* pipes, framed *khanjar* daggers and so on) look out for branches of Al Jaber Gallery and Pride of Kashmir. The best selection of souvenir shops can be found in Souk Madinat Jumeirah and Khan Murjan Souk – items for sale here are generally of a higher quality, albeit at above-average prices. The Camel Company (branches in malls citywide) does an entertaining line in cute toy camels and related merchandise. Gallery One (also with outlets in malls across the city) does a superb range of limited-edition framed art photographs of the region, plus superior postcards.

For items crafted by Dubai-based artisans, browse among the stalls at Marina Market, held at Dubai Marina on Fridays from October to April. The Creative Art Centre, near Jumeira Road, is a treasure-trove of artwork, old maps, antique Arabian jewellery and wooden items from the UAE and Oman.

Original artworks by local artists can be purchased at galleries across the city such as the Majlis and XVA in Bastakiya – although expect to spend some serious cash. Dubai-based artist Susan Walpole has various lines featuring her distinctive Arabian scenes, from notebooks to mouse mats and mugs, at her shop in Jumaira Plaza.

Ramadan

Remember that during the holy month of Ramadan, eating and drinking in public (which includes smoking and chewing gum) are forbidden during daylight hours, and although hotels serve guests food and drink in curtained-off areas, no alcohol is served anywhere until after dark. The city's nightlife also grinds to a halt: live music is banned and clubs close for the duration.

ENTERTAINMENT

Nightlife

Dubai has a vibrant bar and nightclub scene. The busiest evenings tend to be on or around the local weekend (Wednesday, Thursday, Friday), though other nights can be just as busy at venues with 'ladies night' promotions. Dubai doesn't have a nightlife district as such: the best venues – most commonly in hotels or attached to sports and leisure facilities – are spread throughout the city.

Drinking venues divide into two types: the cheery British-style pubs which can be found in most large hotels, and smarter, more style-conscious bars often with live DJs later in the evening. Pubs generally open from noon to around 2am; bars tend to open later, at 6/7pm and stay open until as late as 3am.

Good pubs include the lively **Long's Bar** in the Towers Rotana hotel on Sheikh Zayed Road (with allegedly the longest bar in the Middle East); the **Irish Village** at Dubai Tennis Stadium, with outdoor seating in a pleasant garden; the convivial **Belgium Beer Café** at the Crowne Plaza in Festival City; the **Sherlock Holmes** pub in the Arabian Courtyard hotel near the Dubai Museum in Bur Dubai; and the raucous **Double Decker** pub in the Al Murooj Rotana hotel near Downtown Dubai, designed to resemble an old London bus.

It's Dubai's bars which really steal the show, however. High-rise bars with incredible views are a particular Dubai speciality. Notable venues include the classy **Vu's Bar**, on the 51st floor of the Jumeirah Emirates Towers Hotel; Neos bar, at the top of

The Address Downtown Dubai hotel; the **Skyview Bar** at the Burj al Arab; **Bar 44**, at the top of the Grosvenor House hotel; and the **New Asia Bar** at the Raffles hotel pyramid in Wafi.

Waterfront bars are another big draw. The most memorable is probably **360°**, perched dramatically at the end of a break-water curling out to sea from the Jumeirah Beach Hotel, and offering unbeatable views of the Burj Al Arab and a very cool ambience. **Sho Cho's** at the Dubai Marine Beach Resort and Spa in Jumeirah is another über-cool venue, popular with the city's beautiful people. Down in Dubai Marina, Le Meridien Mina Seyahi's open-air beachside **Barasti Bar** is another peren-nially popular spot, with a refreshing lack of pretension. Back in the city, **The Terrace** at the Park Hyatt hotel has a stylish but laid-back atmosphere and Creek views to kill for.

The Skyview bar at the top of the Burj al Arab

Other places worth hunt-ing out are the **Bahri Bar** at the Mina A'Salam hotel in Madinat Jumeirah, with Arabian styling and sublime Burj al Arab views; the simi-larly styled **Rooftop Bar** at the One&Only Royal Mirage and the spectacular **Buddha Bar** at the Grosvenor House hotel.

There's also a clutch of decent wine bars in the city. The main venue is **The Agency**, with branches in the Emirates Towers Boulevard and Madinat Jumeirah. **Vintage** in Wafi is also good, as is **Oscar's Vine**

Perks for women

Ladies Nights are a Dubai institution. These are usually held on Wednesday, Thursday or, most commonly, Tuesday nights in an attempt to drum up custom during the quieter midweek evenings, with lots of places around the city offering all sorts of deals for women, ranging from a couple of free cocktails up to complimentary champagne all night.

Society, in the Crowne Plaza on Sheikh Zayed Road.

Dubai has several good nightclubs, with guest DJs regularly flown in from Europe and elsewhere. Far and away the biggest is **Chi** (04 337 9471, www.chinightclubdubai.com), next to Al Nasr Leisureland in Oud Metha, with space for over 3,000 revellers. **Trilogy**, at Madinat Jumeirah (tel: 050 366 6917), is another big venue that pulls in big-name international acts, while the recently relaunched **N'Dulge** (formerly The Sanctuary; tel: 04 426 0000) at the Atlantis resort on Palm Jumeirah is another attractive venue, with separate arena, lounge and terrace areas. Swankiest of all is the **Cavalli Club** (tel: 04 332 5555) at the Fairmont Hotel, by the eponymous Italian designer – very posey and very bling. At the opposite end of the scale, the ever-popular **Zinc** at the Crowne Plaza on Sheikh Zayed Road serves up attitude-free clubbing to an eclectic soundtrack.

Smaller venues worth hunting out include **Plan B** at Wafi (tel: 04 324 4777); the chic little **Apartment** at Jumeirah Beach Hotel, one of the longest-running venues in the city; the chintzy little French-styled **Boudoir** at Dubai Marine Beach Resort and Spa; and the Moroccan-themed **Kasbar** at the One&Only Royal Mirage.

Cinema

Dubai has a number of modern, multi-screen cinemas attached to shopping malls showing mainly mainstream Hollywood movies. The city has three IMAX screens, at Ibn Battuta Mall, Zabeel Park, near Trade Centre Roundabout, and the Meydan racecourse. The showing of free double-bills at open-air venues in winter has become popular – try 'Movies Under The Stars' on the Wafi rooftop (October–May, Sundays from 8pm). The highlight of the year is the Dubai International Film Festival, which takes place at Madinat Jumeirah in December and attracts directors, producers and stars from Hollywood, Bollywood and the Middle East.

Live music

As well as attracting old favourites such as Elton John and Lionel Ritchie, Dubai dates are becoming more common on the world-tour schedules of contemporary chart toppers. For further information, check *Time Out Dubai* or the monthly *What's On*.

Big-name acts usually perform at the amphitheatre in **Dubai Media City**; smaller concerts are held at the **Aviation Club** in Garhoud. There's also regular live music at the **Music Room** in the Majestic Hotel in Bur Dubai.

Rooftop bar and wind-tower

Many bars have live music. On Friday evenings in winter, the Wafi rooftop garden hosts the open-air **Peanut Butter Jam** sessions (Oct–May Fri 8pm–midnight), featuring sets by local musicians. Entry is free, and the crowd lounges on bean-bags in front of the stage. Jazz fans are catered to by the annual Dubai International Jazz Festival (January–February); there's also regular jazz at **JamBase** in Souk Madinat Jumeirah; **Up On The 10th** in the Radisson Blu hotel in Deira; and the **Blue Bar**, at the Novotel off Sheikh Zayed Road.

Performing arts

Dubai's first purpose-built theatre at **Madinat Jumeirah** (tel: 04 366 8888) has been slow to develop a full season of entertainment; the same goes for the **Palladium** in Dubai Media City. **Dubai Drama Group** has a permanent home in the Dubai Community Theatre and Arts Centre (tel: 04 341 4777) at Mall of the Emirates, which also hosts English-language touring productions. **The Laughter Factory** has been bringing British comedians to the city for several years.

DUBAI FOR CHILDREN

Most of the large shopping malls have dedicated children's entertainment zones/play areas. At the Dubai Mall you'll find KidZania, where kids get to role-play various jobs, the hi-tech Sega Republic, and the Dubai Aquarium. Other child-centred attractions include **Children's City** and the **WonderLand Theme and Water Park** and **Dubai Dolphinarium** nearby; **Aquaplay** at Mirdif City Centre; and **Stargate**, a space-themed entertainment complex in Zabeel Park.

Wild Wadi waterpark

Kids will also love **Wild Wadi** waterpark, **Ski Dubai**, and the attractions at the **Atlantis** resort – Aquaventure, Dolphin Bay and the Lost Chambers. Most children will also probably enjoy the thrills of a **desert safari** or a trip aboard the **Wonder Bus**.

Calendar of Events

January *Dubai Marathon* Leading long-distance runners come to Dubai. *Dubai 24 Hour* Classic motorsport endurance event at the Autodrome.

January–February *Dubai Shopping Festival* Shops across the city offer massive discounts and special promotions. *Dubai International Jazz Festival* Performances by big-name jazz and pop stars.

January–March *Meydan Races* Main race season at Meydan racecourse.

February *Dubai Desert Classic, Emirates Golf Course* The Middle East's premier golfing tournament, attracting top international players. *RAK Half-Marathon, Ras al Khaimah* Popular half-marathon in northern emirate of RAK.

February–March *Dubai Tennis Championships, Aviation Club* Top male and female players battle it out in Garhoud.

March *Dubai World Cup, Meydan racecourse* The world's richest horse race. *Art Dubai* Huge international art fair. *Bastakiya Art Fair* Fringe alternative to Art Dubai, focusing on Arab artists. *Sharjah Biennial Art Festival* (odd-numbered years only) Prestigious biennial art expo. *Taste of Dubai Food Festival, Dubai Media City* Citywide foodie promotions, plus workshops with leading local and international chefs.

April *Perrier Chill-Out Festival* Laidback music festival with top names. *Womad Abu Dhabi* Abu Dhabi instalment of the world music festival.

June–August *Dubai Summer Surprises* Citywide retail promotions and mall-based entertainment.

October *Abu Dhabi Film Festival* Films from Arabia and beyond.

October–November *Abu Dhabi Desert Challenge* Rally drivers race through the desert.

November *Abu Dhabi F1 Grand Prix, Yas Island*.

December *UAE National Day* (2 December). Dhow races, parades, and traditional music and dance performances. *Dubai World Championship, Jumeirah Golf Estates* Season-ending finale to the European Golf Tour. *Dubai Ladies Masters, Emirates Golf Club* Leading event on Ladies' European Tour. *Dubai Rugby Sevens, The Sevens Stadium* Massively popular rugby tournament. *Dubai International Film Festival, Madinat Jumeirah* Focusing on African, Asian and especially Arab cinema. *ITF Al Habtoor Tennis Challenge, Dubai Marina*.

EATING OUT

You won't go hungry in Dubai – quite the opposite in fact, as the city increasingly consolidates its position as the food capital of the Middle East. As you would expect, the city is a particularly good place to sample Arabian cuisine, but at the culinary crossroads between Europe, Asia and Arabia, it offers a cosmopolitan spread of cuisines, in a huge variety of settings. At the bottom of the scale, you can eat well for just a handful of dirhams at one of the city's streetside *shwarma* stands, inexpensive Lebanese cafés, or in one of the hundreds of bargain-basement curry houses that can be found throughout Bur Dubai and Karama. At the top of the scale, the sky's the limit, with opulent restaurants with world-class chefs in spectacular waterfront or high-rise locations.

Al Muntaha restaurant in the Burj al Arab

Standards at the best places are top-notch, and international celebrity chefs have also been drawn to the city – Gordon Ramsay, Gary Rhodes, Nobu Matsuhisa, Sanjeev Kapoor, Vineet Bhatia, Pierre Gagnaire and the late Santi Santamaria have all opened restaurants in the city (although Ramsay has now departed).

MEAL TIMES

Meals are eaten at the times you'd expect in any international city: breakfast from 6.30 to 9am, lunch between noon and 3pm and dinner not earlier than 8pm. That said, outside the hotels, many cafés and restaurants are open from breakfast to the early hours of the next morning.

The one time of year when the opening hours of cafés and restaurants vary from the norm is during the period of Ramadan, when Muslims fast during daylight hours for a month. Throughout this time, which moves from year to year, even non-Muslims are forbidden to eat, drink or smoke in public between sunrise and sunset. Accordingly, non-hotel restaurants are closed until sunset, though some may keep their kitchens open to serve take-away meals. During the day, it's possible to eat in hotel restaurants that are shielded from view behind wooden screens, but alcohol won't be served until the evening.

Friday brunch

The Dubai Friday brunch is a city institution, equivalent to the British Sunday roast. It is particularly popular amongst the city's European expat set, while many restaurants lay on all-you-can-eat (and sometimes drink, as well) deals. Brunch usually kicks off around midday, and can last for the remainder of the afternoon. Check *Time Out Dubai* for all the latest venues and deals.

WHERE TO EAT

If you want to drink alcohol with your meal, your eating options are immediately restricted to licensed restaurants in hotels – although don't assume that just because a place is unlicensed the food will be below par. Wherever you're going, the best places can get booked up quickly, particularly at weekends; so it pays to reserve.

Outdoor restaurant in
Madinat Jumeirah

Hotels

There's a vast range of different places to eat in the city's myriad hotels, ranging from functional 24-hour coffee shops and buffet restaurants through to ultra-swanky fine-dining palaces. The majority of hotel restaurants are licensed, although there are exceptions. Many of the best places take advantage of their spectacular locations. These include a number of magical beachfront restaurants (such as Pierchic at Al Qasr hotel, or Eauzone at the One&Only Royal Mirage), plus various places in spectacular high-rise locations at (or near) the top of the city's skyscrapers (Vu's Restaurant in the Emirates Towers, Al Muntaha in the Burj al Arab, and At.mosphere in the Burj Khalifa are probably the three best known). Other places take advantage of waterside locations around the city (Thai Kitchen at the Park Hyatt, overlooking the Creek, for example, or Thiptara at The Palace hotel, which overlooks the Dubai Fountain).

For something with a more local flavour, Dubai's hotels are a good place to sample traditional Arabian fare, often with live music and belly-dancing – these places frequently don't get going till late, but stay lively into the small hours. Al Tannour at the Crowne Plaza in Sheikh Zayed Road and Al Qasr at the Dubai Marine Beach Resort are two good spots.

On the street

For a quintessential Dubai meal, nothing beats a simple shwarma, bought at a local café or pavement shwarma stand and eaten at a streetside table watching the crowds go by – a simple, tasty meal for little more than a dollar or two. Slightly more elaborate (but still inexpensive) Arabian food can be found at numerous cafés across the city, most of which will also do a good line in shisha. Good areas for inexpensive Arabian food include the Creekside in the old city centre (Kanzaman in Shindagha is a particular favourite), Sheikh Zayed Road, and Al Diyafah Street in the suburb of Satwa (with Beirut and Al Mallah the two best-known places). The Gulf-wide chain of Automatic restaurants can also be found across the city, offering substantial and very reasonably priced Lebanese cuisine; the local Japengo chain (also with branches citywide) also does good Lebanese as part of its wide-ranging menu. Look out too for branches of the Zaatar w Zeit chain, which offers good Lebanese-style fast food at bargain prices.

Shish kebab skewers

Cheap but well-prepared food can also be found at the innumerable inexpensive Indian and Pakistani cafés dotted across the city. The majority of these can be found in Bur Dubai and in the 'curry corridor' stretching along Sheikh Zayed Road from just past the BurJuman Centre up to Karama. Cafés tend to specialise either in generic North Indian/Pakistani-style meat curries, or in vegetarian cuisine (the international Saravanna Bhavan chain has a number of branches in the city and is particularly good for both North and South Indian vegetarian cooking).

Arabic coffee

Café society

Dubai has its own distinctive café culture – hanging out over coffee and a shisha plays a central role in Arabian culture. Most of the best places have a decidedly local flavour, patronized by Emiratis and expat Arabs and usually with a good shisha selection. More European-style cafés include the popular Lime Tree Café in Jumeirah, the XVA Café and Basta Arts Café in Bastakiya, the funky Dutch-owned More in Garhoud and the DIFC, and the chintzy Shakespeare and Co., with several branches around the city.

Malls and sports clubs

All malls have food courts offering the usual international fast food and chain restaurants, but look out for appealing venues that are located away from the food courts. At Wafi there's the arty European Elements café and the Lebanese deli and restaurant, Wafi Gourmet. At Mercato in Jumeira and the BurJuman Centre in Bur Dubai, there's the French-style Paul boulangerie and café. The classy Australian café chain Dôme has outlets at BurJuman, Jumeira Plaza and Souk Madinat Jumeirah. An alternative to the American and European coffee franchises in Jumeira is Gerard in Magrudy's Mall, a Dubai institution. Almaz by Momo, at Mall of the Emirates, is worth a visit for its sumptuous North African cuisine.

The city's sports clubs also provide a home for a number of perennially popular restaurants. The various Creekside venues (with stunning views) at the Dubai Creek Golf and Yacht Club continue to attract a local clientele, while the nearby Aviation

Club in Garhoud is home to another lively cluster of restaurants. Further south, the sparkling new Dubai Marina Yacht Club, overlooking the Marina, has an appealing selection of places to eat and drink.

Dinner cruises

For a meal with a difference, try one of the dinner cruises on the Creek aboard a traditional wooden dhow. These are offered by pretty much every tour operator in the city and are usually most easily arranged through your hotel. Cruise operators include Rikks Cruises (tel: 04 357 2200, www.rikks.net), which offers some of the cheapest cruises in town, and the more upmarket Al Mansour Dhow, operated by the Radisson Blu hotel (tel: 04 205 7333).

For a modern alternative to the traditional dhow, Bateaux Dubai (tel: 04 399 4994, www.bateauxdubai.com) runs cruises

Shisha pipes

Shisha smoking is a very popular way to round off a meal in many Arabic restaurants. Shisha are free-standing water pipes consisting of a water-filled container topped with tobacco, a small bowl of glowing charcoal and a long pipe with a mouthpiece. It has been nicknamed 'hubble-bubble' in English because of the bubbling sound the water makes as the smoke is drawn through the pipe, but is also known as 'hookah', after *huqqah*, the Arabic word for container, and *nargileh*, which is derived from the Persian word for coconut, *nargil* (coconuts were once used to contain the water).

Shisha can be smoked plain but is usually offered in a range of flavours – anything from apple, strawberry or melon through to fruit cocktail or cappuccino. Aficionados claim that because the smoke is drawn through water it is cleansed of much of its nicotine content. Even so, shisha can be habit-forming, although if you only sample it once or twice you're unlikely to become hooked on the hookah.

in its state-of-the-art glass-sided boat, offering a touch more luxury than other operators, plus better-than-average food. Alternatively, Danat Dubai Cruises (tel: 04 351 1117) run upmarket cruises along the Creek and also out along the coast, aboard their state-of-the-art catamaran.

WHAT TO EAT

Though it is not widely available, Emirati food consists of simple rice, fish or meat dishes, such as *matchbous* (spiced lamb with rice), *hareis* (slow-cooked wheat and lamb) and *fareed* (a meat and vegetable stew poured over thin bread).

Baba Ghanoush and Fatayer Bil Sabanikh as part of a mezze

Sadly Emirati food hardly ever appears on restaurant menus – the best place to try it is usually the Khan Murjan Restaurant in the Khan Murjan Souk.

Traditional Arabian food (often described as 'Lebanese', since many of the most common dishes come from Lebanon) features a spread of hot and/or cold *mezze* (small dishes, like a kind of Middle Eastern tapas) followed by grilled main courses – such as lamb or chicken *shwarma* sliced from a vertical spit, or mixed grills and locally caught fish – served with Arabic bread, French fries or rice. The best places serve up a considerable variety of *mezze*, including hot dishes such as *kebeh* (fried minced lamb with crushed wheat), *sambousek* (samosa-style pastries filled with minced lamb and pine nuts or *haloumi* cheese or spinach), and *arayes* (bread stuffed with minced lamb, tomato and cheese). Cold *mezze* includes hummus, *moutabbal* (a paste of grilled aubergine with *tahini* and lemon), *tabouleh* (a finely chopped parsley salad with mint, fresh tomatoes, onion and crushed wheat, topped with olive oil and lemon), and *fattoush* (a green salad with toasted bread).

Arabic desserts include *kashta* (clotted cream topped with pistachio, pine nuts and honey); and *Umm Ali* (literally, 'Mother of Ali'), a bread and butter pudding with sultanas and coconut, topped with nuts.

Arabic or Lebanese 'fast food' comprises sandwiches made with Arabic bread and a variety of fillings, including *shwarma* or falafel (mashed chickpeas and spices deep fried in flattened balls), served with a salad garnish. Also worth sampling is *manakeesh*, a round, pizza-like bread covered with *zatar*, a mixture of dried thyme, sesame seed, spices and olive oil.

Though the Muslim population is forbidden to eat pork or consume alcohol, both are used as ingredients on hotel menus and are flagged up for those who must abstain. Without exception, all other meat is halal. Non-hotel venues substitute beef, bacon or chicken sausages for pork.

WHAT TO DRINK

Popular beverages throughout the Gulf are *shai* (tea) and *kahwa* (coffee). Traditional Arabian coffee is quite unlike that found in the West; it is served very strong, flavoured with cardamom and other spices, and served in little cups without handles. Tea is widely available, including Indian-style *masala chai*. A fantastic selection of fresh juices is available in Arabic restaurants and at specialist juice stalls.

TO HELP YOU ORDER...

English is widely spoken, so English speakers should not have a problem, particularly in hotels. Arabic-speaking service staff, mostly from the Levant or North Africa, will understand some English, but here are a few Arabic phrases, just in case:

Do you have a table?	**Indaakum towla?**
Is there anyone here who speaks English?	**Haal yoojad ahad yatakaalam al-lugha al-ingleezia?**
May I see the menu, please?	**Laow samaht, ana ureed laeehat ataamm?**
Excuse me.	**Afwan.**
I don't eat meat.	**La akul lahem.**
What do you recommend?	**Maatha tansah?**
May I have the bill, please?	**Fatoura, laow samaht.**
I'd like ...	**Ana ureed...**

thank you	**shukran**	I've finished.	**Ana khallast.**
yes	**nam**	no	**la**
beef	**lahem bakar**	milk	**haleeb**
bread	**khobez**	pepper	**bahar**
chicken	**dajaj**	rice	**rouz**
coffee	**kahwa**	salad	**salata**
dessert	**helou**	salt	**melh**
fish	**samak**	sandwich	**sandweesh**
French fries	**batata makleea**	soup	**shorba**
fruit	**fawakah**	tea	**shai**
ice cream	**booza**	vegetables	**khodra**
lamb	**lahem harouf**	water	**mai**

... AND READ THE MENU

bajella	local variation on boiled foul
esh asaraya	cheesecake with cream topping
foul	fava-bean stew with garlic and lemon

ghuzi	whole roast lamb with rice and pine nuts
hallaweeyat	desserts
jarjir	rocket leaves and onion
kofta	minced lamb with parsley and onion
lahem	meat (not including chicken)
logaimat	fried balls made from egg, flour and saffron
mashawee	grills
mehalabiya	milk custard with pistachios and rosewater
nakhi	boiled chick peas
roub	cucumber with yoghurt
salatat zatar	thyme salad with onions, lemon and olive oil
shish kebab	grilled mutton marinated with cumin and cinnamon
shish tawouq	grilled chicken pieces marinated with cumin and cinnamon
toum	crushed garlic and mayonnaise

Lebanese *kebeh*, a croquette stuffed with minced beef or lamb

PLACES TO EAT

The price categories below are based on the average cost of a meal for two with a glass of wine each in hotel venues, or soft drinks elsewhere.

$$$$$** More than Dhs500   **$$$$ Dhs400–500
$$$** Dhs200–400   **$$ Dhs100–200
$ Less than Dhs100

DUBAI

THE COAST

Al Mahara $$$$$ *Burj Al Arab, Umm Suqeim, tel: 04 301 7600*. Centred on an enormous fishtank, this subterranean seafood restaurant is one of Dubai's most expensive. Men are expected to wear a jacket at dinner; no jeans. Open daily 12.30–3pm and 7pm–midnight.

Amala $$$$ *Jumeirah Zabeel Saray, The Palm Jumeirah, tel: 04 453 0444*. Recently opened Indian fine-dining restaurant in the new Jumeirah Zabeel Saray hotel, this place has had rave reviews for its opulent décor and superb classical North Indian cooking – and the set-price dinner at 225dh is a good deal. Daily 6pm–1am.

Buddha Bar $$$$ *Grosvenor House, Dubai Marina, tel: 04 317 6000*. One of the best-looking restaurants in Dubai, with a fine array of Japanese, Thai and Chinese mains. Open daily 7.30pm–midnight.

Indego $$$$ *Grosvenor House Hotel, tel: 04 399 8888*. Overseen by Vineet Bhatia, India's first Michelin-starred chef, this stylish restaurant showcases Bhatia's outstanding 'contemporary Indian' cooking, with international ingredients and techniques. Open Sun–Thurs 7pm–midnight.

Japengo $$ *Palm Strip Shopping Mall, Jumeira Road, tel: 04 345 4979*. Chic café-restaurant, with an eclectic menu featuring everything from sushi and sashimi through to stir-fries, pizzas, pastas, *mezze* and lamb chops, plus sandwiches and salads. There is another branch overlooking the canal in the Souk Madinat Jumeirah. Open Fri–Wed 10am–1am, Thur 10am–2am.

Lime Tree Café $–$$ *Jumeira Road, tel: 04 349 8498.* Set in an attractive modern villa, this neat café offers a classic slice of expat Jumeirah life. Healthy specialities include tasty wraps, delicious smoothies and the best carrot cake in Dubai. Open daily 7.30am–6pm.

Nina $$$$ *Arabian Courtyard, One&Only Royal Mirage, tel: 04 399 9999.* Innovative modern Indian restaurant, combining subcontinental flavours with international ingredients and cooking techniques – anything from traditional butter chicken through to frogs' legs and *rambutan.* Open Mon–Sat 7–11.30pm.

Pai Tai $$$$ *Al Qasr hotel, Madinat Jumeirah, tel: 04 366 6730.* One of the city's most romantic places to eat, with live music and stunning Burj Al Arab views from the candlelit terrace. The menu features Thai classics, including spicy salads and meat and seafood curries. Licensed. Dress: smart casual. Open daily 6.30–11.30pm.

Pierchic $$$$$ *Al Qasr hotel, Madinat Jumeirah, tel: 04 366 6730.* A fabulous seafood venue at the end of a wooden pier with stunning views of the Madinat Jumeirah resort and Burj Al Arab. Open daily 1–3pm and 7–11.30pm.

Rhodes Mezzanine $$$$$ *Grosvenor House Hotel, tel: 04 399 8888.* Dubai outpost of UK celebrity chef Gary Rhodes, with a short but inventive menu showcasing modern European cuisine, accompanied by classic British puddings like jam roly poly and bread-and-butter pudding. Open Mon–Sat 7–11.30pm.

Tagine $$$ *One&Only Royal Mirage, Al Sufouh Road, tel: 04 399 9999.* Exquisitely decorated little Moroccan restaurant with Arabian Nights décor and a fine array of traditional Moroccan cuisine, including tagines and traditional dishes like spicy harira soup, lamb's brain and pigeon pie. Open Tue–Sun 7–11.30pm.

Zheng He's $$$$ *Mina A'Salam, Madinat Jumeirah, tel: 04 366 6730.* One of the top Chinese restaurants in Dubai, with sumptuous décor and superb classic and contemporary Chinese fare, including excellent dim sum. Open daily noon–3pm and 7–11.30pm.

SHEIKH ZAYED ROAD

Almaz by Momo $$$ *Harvey Nichols, Mall of the Emirates, Sheikh Zayed Road, tel: 04 409 8877.* Dubai version of the celebrity hangout in London, offering mezze and traditional Moroccan mains in a contemporary North African-themed interior. Open Sat–Thur 10am–midnight, Fri 10am–1.30am.

Al Nafoorah $$$ *Emirates Towers Boulevard, tel: 04 319 8088.* The best Lebanese restaurant in town, with beautifully prepared hot and cold mezze, grills and a good wine list, including Lebanese vintages. Open daily 12.30–3pm and 8pm–12.30am.

At.mosphere $$$$$ *Burj Khalifa, Downtown Dubai, tel: 04 888 3828.* At.mosphere is the world's highest bar and restaurant, located on the 122nd floor of the soaring Burj Khalifa, the world's tallest building. Choose between The Lounge for a drink, light meal or pricey afternoon tea and The Grill, offering upmarket steaks in its svelte dining room. The Grill daily 12.30–3pm and 7–11.30pm; The Lounge daily noon–2am.

The Exchange Grill $$$$$ *Fairmont Hotel, Sheikh Zayed Rd, tel: 04 311 8559.* The city's most exclusive steakhouse, this small and very upmarket establishment serves choice Gold Angus and Wagyu cuts, backed by one of the city's most extensive wine lists. Open Sun–Thurs 12.30–3.30pm and 7pm–midnight, Fri and Sat 7pm–midnight.

The Noodle House $$ *Emirates Towers Boulevard, tel: 04 319 8758.* Popular Asian fusion restaurant with bench and table seating that is crowded with office workers at lunchtimes. Open daily noon–midnight.

Spectrum On One $$$$ *Fairmont hotel, tel: 04 311 8101.* A stylish restaurant in a hip hotel serving good food from eight separate open kitchens – Chinese, Japanese, Arabian, Indian, European, etc. Open daily 7pm–1am.

Teatro $$$ *Towers Rotana, tel: 04 343 8000.* Serving five different cuisines, this lively restaurant has a theatrical theme without pretensions. Open daily 6pm–2am.

Thiptara $$$$$ *The Palace – The Old Town, Downtown Burj Dubai, tel: 04 428 7961.* This beautiful Thai restaurant is set in a traditional wooden pavilion jutting out into the waters of the lake behind the Dubai Mall, with peerless views of the Burj Khalifa and Dubai Fountain. The menu concentrates on sumptuous Bangkok-style seafood, plus meat and veg options. Open daily 7pm–midnight.

Vu's $$$$ *Jumeirah Emirates Towers Hotel, tel: 04 319 8088.* Inventive fusion fine-dining on the 50th floor of the landmark Jumeirah Emirates Towers hotel. A mix of European and Asian influences, plus stunning views. Lunch set menus are affordable, evening a la carte is pricey. Open daily 12.30–3pm and 7.30pm–midnight.

Zuma $$$$ *The Gate Village 06, DIFC, tel: 04 425 5660.* This über-chic bar-restaurant is a hit both with Dubai's fashionistas and local foodies, thanks to its cool ambience and excellent range of classic and contemporary Japanese fare – Friday brunches (with live DJ) are particularly popular. Restaurant open Sat–Wed 12.30–3pm, Thurs 12.30–3pm and 7pm–1am, Fri 12.30–3.30pm and 7pm–1am; lounge and bar open daily midnight–2am (Thurs until 3am).

BUR DUBAI

Bastakiah Nights $$$ *Bastakiya, tel: 04 353 7772.* Good Arabic and Iranian food served in a wonderful traditional wind-towered house. Open daily 12.30–11.30pm.

Chhappan Bhog $ *Sheikh Khalifa Bin Zayed Road (Trade Centre Road), Karama, tel: 04 396 8176.* A friendly Indian restaurant specialising in vegetarian *thalis*, with dishes that are regularly refilled. Open daily 12.30–2.30pm and 8–11.30pm.

Kan Zaman $$ *Shindagha, tel: 04 393 9913.* In a fine location near the mouth of the Creek, Kan Zaman has breezy outdoor and waterside seating and a good selection of Lebanese mezze, Turkish coffee and shisha. Open daily 6pm–1.30pm.

Ravi's $ *Near Satwa Roundabout, tel: 04 331 5353.* This legendary little café remains popular with locals, expats and tourists alike for its cheap and tasty Pakistani-style chicken, mutton and veg curries, while the outdoor seating offers a good (if noisy) perch from which to enjoy the passing street life. Open daily 10am–11pm.

DEIRA

Asha's $$$ *Wafi, Oud Metha, tel: 04 324 4100.* Owned by legendary Bollywood chanteuse Asha Bhosle, this smart Wafi restaurant offers Indian classics alongside more unusual regional specialities, including recipes from Asha's own cookbook. Open daily 12.30–3pm and 7.30–midnight.

Ashiana Sheraton $$$ *Dubai Creek, Baniyas Road, tel: 04 207 1733.* One of Dubai's oldest upmarket Indian restaurants, but the most consistent, specialising in hearty North Indian cuisine in rich and flavoursome sauces. Live music. Open Sun–Thurs noon–3pm & 7.30–11.30pm, Fri and Sat 7.30–11.30pm.

Blue Elephant $$$ *Al Bustan Rotana Hotel, Garhoud, tel: 04 282 0000.* One of Dubai's best Thai restaurants, located in a quaint Thai-style 'village'. Open Mon–Sat noon–3pm and 7pm–midnight.

The Boardwalk $$ *Dubai Creek Golf and Yacht Club, tel: 04 295 6000.* The mainstream menu of international food is reliable enough, but it's the terrific views from the outdoor seating on the restaurant's boardwalk that steal the show. Open Sun–Thurs noon–midnight, Fri and Sat 8am–midnight.

Focaccia $$$ *Hyatt Regency, Corniche Road, Deira, tel: 04 209 1234.* Upmarket but pleasantly casual Italian restaurant, with Gulf views and a good range of traditional and modern Italian cuisine, with a seasonally changing menu. Daily 7pm–midnight, also Fri brunch 12:30pm to 4pm.

More $$ *Behind Lifco Supermarket, near Welcare Hospital, Garhoud, tel: 04 283 0224.* A funky Dutch-owned bistro with a wide range of superior international café fare. Difficult to beat for its combination of excellent atmosphere, value and service. Open daily 8am–10pm.

Reflets Par Pierre Gagnaire $$$$$ *InterContinental Dubai, Festival City, tel: 04 701 1111.* Arguably Dubai's top restaurant, showcasing Pierre Gagnaire's innovative contemporary French cooking, served with enormous panache. Open Sun–Fri 7–11pm.

Shabestan $$$–$$$$ *Radisson Blu, Baniyas Rd, tel: 04 222 7171.* Perhaps the best Iranian restaurant in the city, specialising in huge *chelo* kebabs, fish stews and other Persian specialities, accompanied by an Iranian band of violin, drum and santour (nightly except Sat). Open daily 12.30–3pm and 7–11pm.

Table 9 $$$$ *Hilton Dubai Creek, tel: 04 227 1111.* Formerly Gordon Ramsay's Verre, this outstanding restaurant has recently relaunched under his former protégés Nick Alvis and Scott Price, offering the same top-notch modern European fine-dining, but with a more flexible menu, relaxed ambience and lower prices. Signature creations like the house liquorice meringue and crispy egg have already won rave reviews. Daily 7pm–midnight.

The Thai Kitchen $$$$ *Park Hyatt, Garhoud, tel: 04 317 2222.* One of the best and most romantic Thai restaurants in town, set on the Park Hyatt's idyllic Creekside terrace and offering a sumptuous range of unusual regional specialities. Licensed. Dress: smart casual. Open daily 7pm–midnight, also Friday brunch 12.30–4pm.

A–Z TRAVEL TIPS

A Summary of Practical Information

A

ACCOMMODATION

There's a huge range of accommodation in Dubai, including innumerable five-stars, although good accommodation lower down the price scale is more difficult to find. The cheapest accommodation is in the numerous one- and two-star hotels around the old city centre in Bur Dubai and Deira, although even here you'll struggle to find a room for less than US$75 a night. Rates at the city's more upmarket hotels start at around US$150 a night, rising to as much as US$2000 a night. For beach hotels it pays to reserve as far ahead as possible.

Dubai's high season runs roughly from October through to April. The low season stretches through the hotter months of May to August, during which prices can fall significantly.

AIRPORT

Dubai International Airport, otherwise known as DXB (tel: 04 216 2525, www.dubaiairport.com), is centrally located on the Deira side of Dubai Creek, in Garhoud and Al Qusais districts. There are three terminals. The sparkling new Terminal 3 is where all Emirates flights arrive and depart. Terminal 1 handles other long-haul international flights, while Terminal 2 handles short-haul flights. Both Terminals 1 and 3 have their own dedicated metro stations, and there are plentiful taxis, although note that these charge a rip-off Dhs 20 surcharge when picking up from the airport. Numerous buses also service the airport, although few of these go anywhere very useful, from a visitor's point of view. ATMs, money-exchange bureaux and car-hire desks can be found in all three terminals.

ALCOHOL

Dubai has a relatively liberal attitude to the consumption of alcohol by non-Muslims as long as it is limited to licensed premises and people do not drink and drive. Beers, wines and spirits are readily available in hotels (rooms, restaurants and bars) and clubs, but not, generally, anywhere else. Alcohol is not sold in supermarkets and only residents with government-issued liquor licences can buy from licensed vendors MMI and A&E.

Dubai has a zero-tolerance approach to drink-driving and offenders face a lengthy legal process, three weeks in prison and even deportation, whatever the amount of alcohol detected in the blood. Note that you risk arrest if driving the morning after a heavy night if there is still any trace of alcohol in your system. Being drunk and disorderly in public is also an offence, as is buying alcohol for a Muslim. The sale of alcohol everywhere is restricted during the Islamic holy month of Ramadan.

Finally, visitors should remember that the effects of alcohol are exacerbated by heat and humidity. To avoid dehydration, make sure you drink plenty of water.

B

BUDGETING FOR YOUR TRIP

Shop around for the best deals on flights and accommodation as there are lots of good value packages available. Dubai is an expensive place for visitors, though eating out (in cheaper restaurants) and travelling around using public transport needn't be too costly.

Travelling to Dubai. Combination airfare–hotel deals are often cheaper than separately arranged air travel and accommodation. The best prices are low season (May–Sept), but that's the hottest time of the year in the UAE. As a very rough guide, packages from the UK, based on two adults and including economy-class airfare and five nights in a deluxe room at a five-star hotel, with airport transfers and breakfast, start from around £1,500 in high season, £1,200 in low season.

Accommodation. If you're not on a package deal, the cost for a standard double room ranges from around Dhs300–350 per night in a one-star hotel up to around Dhs750 at the cheapest five-star hotel through to around Dhs10,000 per night for a suite at the seven-star Burj Al Arab.

Meals and drinks. It's possible to eat for as little as Dhs15 per person if you go for a shwarma sandwich in a street-side café or a curry in a no-nonsense Indian or Pakistani outlet. Main courses in most decent Western-style, non-hotel restaurants are Dhs25–50. For fine dining, budget for upwards of Dhs70 per person for main courses. Cans of soft drinks start at Dhs2 in shops, but are marked up by as much as 800 percent in restaurants. Freshly made juices cost Dhs6–15. A tall caffè latte at Starbucks costs Dhs15. Imported alcoholic drinks are generally the same price or more expensive than they would be in the West.

Local transport. Transport is cheap if you stick to public transport: tickets on the Dubai Metro and buses start from Dhs3.5, while the trip across the Creek by abra (water taxi) costs just Dhs1. Taxis are reasonably priced, too, with a minimum charge of Dhs10 and a cost of around Dhs1.6 per kilometre (although taxis picked up at the airport have a Dhs20 surcharge). A taxi from the airport to Deira or Bur Dubai will cost around Dhs40–50; considerably more (Dhs80–100) to the more distant resort hotels along the Jumeira coast. Many hotels offer a free airport transfer service. The ordinary fare for taxis between the resort hotels and the city centre is around Dhs80–100 one way, so consider taking the shuttle buses provided by most hotels.

A half-day desert safari with a tour company costs around Dhs250–350. The price of petrol is around Dhs6 per imperial gallon for unleaded Special (95 octane).

C

CAR HIRE

Hiring a car is one of the best ways to explore the city and emirate of Dubai. Car-hire companies include Avis (www.avisuae.ae/Contact.aspx), **Budget** (www.budget-uae.com/rentallocations.aspx), **Thrifty** (www.thriftyuae.com/contact.asp), **Europcar** (www.europcar-middleeast.com), Hertz (www.hertzuae.com/content/ourlocation.aspx) and

Sixt (www.sixt-uae.com/en/location), with numerous offices citywide – see the websites for details of office locations. The cheapest cars start from under Dhs100 a day, including insurance and unlimited mileage.

Most national driving licences are recognised, but it's a good idea to have a valid international driving licence with you as back-up in case the rules change. For insurance reasons, visitors can only drive rental cars and not privately owned vehicles. To drive a resident friend's car, for example, visitors must get a temporary licence from Dubai Police.

CLIMATE

Dubai is an arid, desert nation with mild, pleasant winters and very hot, humid summers. While the country enjoys year-round sunshine, the reality is that you can't be out in the sun for long periods in the summer. The period from May to September is particularly hot, with temperatures topping 48°C (118°F) during the day, with around 90 percent humidity.

From October to April, however, the weather is glorious, with monthly averages between 22°C (71°F) and 32°C (90°F), and lows of 10°C (50°F) (evenings can be quite chilly). Humidity also falls considerably at this time of year. Weather-wise, this is undoubtedly the best time to visit, but commensurate with the fall in temperatures is a rise in accommodation costs. What rain there is (127mm/5ins fell in 2008) tends to fall on isolated days between October and March, when heavy morning fog can also occur.

CLOTHING

While swimming trunks and bikinis are fine at the beach (though going topless is not an option anywhere), they are not acceptable in other public areas, such as residential neighbourhoods near beaches, or in souks and malls. It's fine to expose arms and legs, and it's increasingly acceptable for women to bare their shoulders, but shorts and skirts shouldn't ride too high. Generally, men and women are expected to dress modestly, particularly during the Muslim holy month of Ramadan.

Dubai is hot in summer and warm in winter, so lightweight cottons and linens are advisable. Winter evenings can be surprisingly cool, so pack a cardigan or jumper, particularly if you want to enjoy an alfresco evening meal.

CRIME AND SAFETY

Crime is relatively rare in Dubai. Generally, visitors won't encounter criminal activity and need not be concerned about being extra cautious with their possessions. Most people feel safe on the city streets even late at night. Certainly, there are no neighbourhoods to avoid or gangs of rabble-rousing youths to steer clear of. However, follow your usual precautions and make sure you get comprehensive travel and medical insurance before travelling.

You are actually much more likely to fall foul of the law yourself in Dubai than to be the victim of crime – a recent study showed that British nationals were more likely to be arrested in the UAE than in any other country in the world. The range of possible offences includes possession of drugs (even microscopic quantities, or in one's bloodstream on arrival) and traffic-related offences (drink-driving particularly), through to apparently harmless actions such as kissing in public or gesturing at fellow motorists who have annoyed you. Note that many drugs available over the counter or on prescription in the West are illegal in Dubai. Homosexuality is also illegal, although prosecution of Westerners is extremely rare.

The US-led 'war on terror' has led to increased concerns for the safety of citizens of countries associated with American military activity in the region. The UAE is no exception and vigilance against terrorism is recommended.

Call Dubai Police's **Department for Tourist Security** on 800 4438.

CUSTOMS AND ENTRY REQUIREMENTS

Non-renewable 30-day visas are available free on arrival at Dubai International Airport for visitors from 39 countries, including the UK, Ireland, the United States, Canada, Australia, New Zealand, most of Europe and selected Asian nations. For details of longer visas, see http://dubaitourism.ae/definitely-dubai/entry-formalities. Those who don't qualify for a visa on arrival, including South African citizens, can get a 30-day, non-renewable tourist visa through a hotel or tour operator sponsor. This should be arranged before entry to the UAE: visitors should ensure they have a fax copy of the visa with them and they should stop to collect the original at a designated desk in the airport before they head for passport control. The total cost is Dhs 430.

The duty-free allowance for arrivals in Dubai is four litres of alcohol (or 12 cans of beer), 400 cigarettes or 0.5kg of tobacco.

D

DRIVING (See also Car Hire)

Traffic drives on the right-hand side of the road in Dubai (and in the rest of the UAE), so vehicles are left-hand drive. The speed limits on most city streets are 60–80kph (37–50mph), and 100–120kph (62–75mph) on main highways. On road signs, distances are indicated in kilometres.

The road system in the UAE is good, but the general standard of driving can be impatient and aggressive. Accidents are common and the UAE has one of the highest traffic-accident death rates in the world. Lane discipline is poor, so on roads with more than a single lane in one direction, drivers should be aware of what's happening behind and on either side of them before manoeuvring. The fact that major arteries are under radar surveillance seems not to deter high-speed driving. Also bear in mind that around the city, taxi drivers have a nasty habit of swerving, stopping suddenly and blocking traffic if they spot a fare at the roadside, so keep a safe distance behind.

Outside Dubai, particularly on the Hatta highway, there's a possibility of camels wandering onto roads, so be cautious, particularly at night.

Seat belts are compulsory for drivers and front-seat passengers in the UAE, and children under 10 are not allowed to sit in the front passenger seat.

In the city, parking is in designated paid parking zones – look for the orange signs and solar-powered meters. The cost is Dhs1–2 per hour, depending on the area. The fine for not displaying a valid ticket starts at Dhs100. Speeding fines start from Dhs200. Sheikh Zayed Road between Garhoud Bridge and Interchange 4 is a toll road, as is Maktoum Bridge. If you are involved in a road accident, stop and wait for the police. A police report on every level of accident is required for insurance claims. If you are stopped by the police at any time, you must be able to produce your driving licence and car hire/insurance papers (originals, not copies) there and then.

Unless you are an experienced off-road driver, you should not consider hiring a four-wheel drive to head into the harsh and difficult terrain of the desert outside Dubai.

E

ELECTRICITY

The mains electricity in Dubai is 220/240 volts and 50 cycles. Wall sockets are designed for British-type, 13-amp three-pin plugs. Adaptors for two-pin appliances are available in supermarkets.

EMBASSIES AND CONSULATES

As Abu Dhabi, not Dubai, is the federal capital of the UAE, Dubai tends to have foreign consulates, rather than embassies. The telephone numbers for selected countries are:

Australia: 04 508 7100
Canada: 04 314 5555

Ireland: +966 1 488 2300 (Riyadh, Kingdom of Saudi Arabia)
New Zealand: +966 1 488 7988 (Riyadh, Kingdom of Saudi Arabia)
South Africa: 02 447 3446 (Abu Dhabi)
United Kingdom: 04 309 4444
United States: 04 311 6000

EMERGENCIES

Dial 999 for police or ambulance, or 997 for fire.

G

GETTING THERE

Most visitors arrive at Dubai International Airport, though cruise ships dock at Dubai Cruise Terminal in Port Rashid. Alternatively, it is possible to fly into the neighbouring emirates of Abu Dhabi and Sharjah and cross into Dubai by road. The journey from Abu Dhabi takes around ninety minutes to two hours. Sharjah is closer, but in rush-hour traffic the journey can take up to an hour.

Dubai's airport is the major Gulf hub for international air travel, with numerous connections worldwide. There are currently nonstop flights to Dubai from London with Emirates, British Airways, Virgin and Royal Brunei Airlines, and numerous one-stop options with several European and Asian carriers and also with Etihad, Qatar Airways and Gulf Air. Emirates also fly nonstop to Dubai from a number of regional UK airports. From the US, there are a few nonstop flights with Emirates, plus one-stop options with a range of other North American carriers.

The flying time from London to Dubai, direct, is about seven hours.

GUIDES AND TOURS (See also Tourist Information)

Half-day **city sightseeing tours** organised by tour companies combine the main heritage sights with the city's striking modern architecture. An alternative is a hop-on, hop-off ticket with the Big Bus

Company (tel: 04 340 7709, www.bigbustours.com), which operates open-top, double-decker buses daily on city and beach routes. To view Dubai from both the highway and the Creek, take the amphibious Wonder Bus, operated by Wonder Bus Tours (tel: 04 359 5656, www.wonderbusdubai.net), which departs three times daily from the BurJuman Centre in Bur Dubai.

The Sheikh Mohammed Centre for Cultural Understanding (tel: 04 353 6666, www.cultures.ae) runs **walking tours** of historic Bastakiya at 10am on Sundays and Thursdays, and tours of Jumeira Mosque on Saturdays, Sundays, Tuesdays and Thursdays, beginning at 10am. The centre also organises visits to the homes of Emirati families.

Other tours include **desert safaris** and other desert trips, dhow cruises and tours of neighbouring emirates, as well as other activities, from fishing trips to helicopter rides. The leading local tour company is Arabian Adventures, a subsidiary of Emirates airline (tel: 04 303 4888, www.arabian-adventures.com. Other reliable operators include Alpha Tours (tel: 04 294 9888, www.alphatoursdubai.com), Net Tours (tel: 04 602 8888, www.nettoursdubai.com) and Orient Tours (tel: 04 282 8238, www.orient tours.ae).

For details of dhow tours and trips by helicopter or hot-air balloon, see page 85.

H

HEALTH AND MEDICAL CARE

The number to dial for an ambulance is 999. There are good government hospitals as well as numerous private clinics. The main emergency hospital is the government-run Rashid Hospital (tel: 04 337 4000) near Maktoum Bridge in Bur Dubai; emergency treatment is free here. A consultation with a doctor in non-emergency cases costs around Dhs100. For emergencies with children, Al Wasl Hospital (tel: 04 324 1111), across the highway from Wafi City, is a renowned paediatric hospital.

Dental problems can be dealt with by the American Dental Clinic (tel: 04 344 0668, www.american-dental-clinic.com) or the Swedish Dental Clinic (tel: 04 223 1297, www.swedishdental clinic.net).

L

LANGUAGE

Arabic is the official language in the UAE, but English is widely spoken. It is unlikely that you will encounter any difficulty using English in hotels, restaurants or shops, as many of the staff are not Arabic-speakers themselves. That said, wherever you meet someone you know is an Arabic-speaker, it would be polite to have a few words and phrases committed to memory.

hello	**marhaba**
welcome	**ahlan wa-sahlan (ahlan)**
peace be with you (greeting)	**as-salaam alaykum**
and with you be peace (response)	**wa-alaykum as-salaam**
good morning	**sabah al khayr**
good morning (response)	**sabah al nour**
good evening	**masaa al khayr**
good evening (response)	**masaa al nour**
My name is...	**ana ismi...**
What is your name?	**shou ismac?**
How are you?	**kayf haalak?**
well	**zein**
please	**min fadlak**
thank you	**shukran**
yes/no	**naam/la**
finished (as in I have ... or it is ...)	**khallas**
goodbye, peace be with you	**maa as-salaama**

M

MONEY

The currency in Dubai is the UAE dirham (Dhs or AED), which is pegged to the US dollar at the rate of Dhs3.675 to US$1. There are 100 fils in a dirham. The notes in circulation are Dhs 5, 10, 20, 50, 100, 200, 500 and 1,000. Be warned that the brown Dhs1,000 note looks a lot like Dhs200. Generally, it's good to carry Dhs100 notes and lower values for day-to-day transactions. The most common coins are the silver Dhs1, 50 fils and 25 fils.

Banks are generally open Sat–Thur 8am–1pm, closed Fri. The best places to change foreign currency and traveller's cheques into dirhams, however, are the numerous exchanges found in malls and souks, which keep shop hours. The main chains are Al Ansari Exchange (tel: 04 397 7787), Al Fardan Exchange (tel: 04 228 0004), and Thomas Cook Al Rostamani (tel: 04 332 7444). Hotels may exchange cash and traveller's cheques at non-competitive rates for guests.

Major international credit and debit cards are accepted in large shops, restaurants and hotels. When shopping in souks, it's better to bargain for the 'best price' with cash.

O

OPENING HOURS

While Thursday afternoon and Friday are the weekend in the Islamic world, the local weekend in Dubai is Fri–Sat. Friday equates to a Sunday in the West. Banks and many private companies keep business hours on Saturdays.

Generally, government ministries and departments, most embassies and consulates are open Sun–Thur 7.30am–2.30pm; closed Fri–Sat. Many private-sector companies now follow the Western working hours of 9am–6pm, though some offices stick to the traditional split shift, with an extended lunch break between 1 and 4pm; these businesses start earlier, at 8am and close later, at 7pm. During Ramadan, fasting Muslims take a shorter working day and some businesses change their hours accordingly.

P

PHOTOGRAPHY

Visitors should ask permission before taking photos of Emiratis in national dress. Generally, Emirati women do not like having their picture taken, even when covered. The best place to photograph local men and women is the Heritage and Diving Village in Dubai or at Hatta Heritage Village, where they are used to the attention. Note that you should not take photos of government buildings or military bases, and that photography is not allowed at Dubai International Airport.

POLICE

Dubai's police force has a low-key but visible presence in the emirate – its green and white BMW and Mercedes patrol cars are a common sight on the main highways and in residential neighbourhoods. During rush hour, the traffic flow at busy intersections is often managed by police motorcyclists. The emergency number for the police is 999. The toll-free number for general information, including details about the force's Department for Tourist Security, is 800 4438. The police website is www.dubai police.gov.ae.

POST OFFICES

Dubai's Central Post Office (Sat–Thur 8am–8pm, Fri 5–9pm) is located on Zabeel Road in Karama. There are smaller post offices scattered around the city, including Deira (near the Avari Hotel), Satwa (near Ravi's restaurant), Jumeira (on Al Wasl Road) and at Dubai airport. The cost of sending an airmail letter to Western countries is around Dhs5–7 and a postcard around Dhs2–3. Allow 10 days for delivery. International courier companies operating in Dubai include DHL (tel: 800 4004), FedEx (tel: 800 4050) and UPS (tel: 800 4774).

PUBLIC HOLIDAYS

There are eight public holidays in Dubai. Two fall on fixed dates, the others move date year-on-year according to the Islamic calendar, shifting by (usually) 11 days each year.

New Year's Day   Jan 1
UAE National Day   Dec 2

Moveable holidays

Moloud (Prophet Mohammed's Birthday)
Lailat Al Mi'Raj (Ascent of the Prophet)
Eid Al Fitr (end of Ramadan)
Eid Al Adha (Feast of the Sacrifice)
Al Hijra (Islamic New Year)
Ashura (Death of Hussain)

PUBLIC TRANSPORT

Almost all public transport in Dubai – metro, buses and waterbuses (but not *abras*) is covered by the Nol integrated ticket system (www.nol.ae). You will need to get a pre-paid Nol card before you can use any of these. Cards can be bought (or topped up) at any metro station, at numerous bus stops, or at branches of Carrefour, Spinneys, Waitrose and the Emirates NBD Bank. There are four different types of card/ticket. The Red Ticket has been specially designed for visitors, costing just Dhs2, although this has to be topped up with the correct fare before each journey and can only be recharged ten times; you might prefer to invest in a more flexible Silver Card (Dhs20, including Dhs14 credit), which stores up to Dhs500 of credit and lasts five years.

Metro Dubai's new state-of-the-art Metro system (www.rta.ae) has revolutionized travel within the city since opening in 2009, making getting around far easier – and cheaper – than before. The system comprises a mix of overground and underground lines, with bright modern stations, although the popularity of the system means that it is often surprisingly difficult to get a seat. The Metro made history in 2012 when the Middle East's first woman driver started work.

There are two lines currently open. The Red Line runs from Rashidiya via the airport and old city and then down through Karama and along Sheikh Zayed Road all the way to Jebel Ali, at the far southern edge of the city. The Green Line loops around the old city centre through Deira and Bur Dubai. Trains run approximately every 10 minutes from 6am–11pm Sat–Thurs (2pm–midnight on Fridays). Fares start at around Dhs2 up to Dhs7 in standard class, or from around Dhs4 to Dhs14 in the superior Gold Class, which offers slightly plusher carriages.

Bus Catering mainly to the needs of lower-income expat workers, Dubai's bus service is not generally very useful for trips within the city for visitors. For trips to other emirates, there are regular and reliable services from Al Ghubaibah Bus Station in Bur Dubai to Abu Dhabi, Al Ain, Sharjah and (less frequently) Hatta.

Taxi This remains the best way of getting around the areas of the city that the metro has not yet reached. Cabs are metered, air-conditioned, mostly reliable and can be flagged down on the street, or pre-booked. Taxis from the airport start with the meter at Dhs20, though in the city, meters start at Dhs3. The main operators are Dubai Taxi (tel: 04 208 0808), Cars Taxis (tel: 04 800 269 2900), Metro Taxi (tel: 04 600 267 3222) and National Taxis (tel: 04 600 339 0002). Note that street names are rarely used in Dubai except for the biggest roads, and navigation is usually by local landmarks – which is how taxi drivers will expect to be directed, rather than being given a street address, which will most likely mean nothing to them.

Waterbus or **Abra** Dubai is split in two by the Creek, which can be crossed (most memorably) by *abra* or, alternatively, waterbus. Air-conditioned waterbuses serve various points on the Creek, costing Dhs4 per return journey (no single fares available), payable only with a Nol card. They're much less enjoyable than the city's *abras*, however, and at double the price have little to recommend them.

R

RELIGION

Islam is the official religion of the UAE, but there is freedom of worship for Christians in church compounds, on the understanding that they do not proselytise. The main church services are held on Friday – the local weekend. Bibles for personal use can be carried into the country.

All Muslims, except young children, the elderly and pregnant women, observe Ramadan, which lasts 29 or 30 days each year. During this month they abstain from food and drink (and smoking and sex) from sunrise to sunset. Most hotel restaurants will serve food to visitors during the daytime (often screening tables from public view) but you should be sensitive not to eat or drink (or chew gum) in public during this holy month.

The dates for Ramadan move each year, following the Islamic calendar.

T

TELEPHONE

The international dialling code for the UAE is 00 971. The code for Dubai landlines is 04 – overseas callers should drop the 0. Calls within Dubai are free. The code for UAE mobile phones is 050 or 055 – again, overseas callers should drop the first 0.

The local telecoms provider, Etisalat (tel: 101 or 144), provides international direct dialling to 170 countries. The code for dialling internationally is 00. Etisalat payphones (card- or coin-operated) can be found in malls, usually near the prayer room or toilet area. It is possible to call internationally on these public phones.

Pre-paid phone cards are available from Etisalat, supermarkets and service stations. Roaming mobile users will gain access to the local GSM service. The number for directory enquiries is 181, where assistance is provided in English as well as Arabic. Automated answering systems in Dubai tend to begin in Arabic, so hold for instructions in English.

TIME DIFFERENCE

Dubai is four hours ahead of GMT/Universal Coordinated Time (UCT), throughout the year.

New York	London	**Dubai**	Jo'burg	Sydney	Auckland
3am	8am	**noon**	10am	7pm	9pm

TIPPING

Tipping is appreciated, but not expected. A 10 percent service charge is often added automatically to bills, although this is not necessarily shared with staff – better to leave cash if you wish to express your appreciation. Tipping in taxis is not expected, although many visitors often round up the fare and let the driver keep the change.

TOILETS

Western-style toilets are commonly found in hotels and restaurants. In malls and other public gathering places there is usually a combination of Western-style and squat toilets.

TOURIST INFORMATION (See also Guides and Tours)

The Government of Dubai Department of Tourism and Commerce Marketing (DTCM; tel: 04 223 0000, www.dubaitourism.ae) is the emirate's official tourism promotion organization. DTCM's information centres in Dubai include kiosks in Terminals 1 and 3 at Dubai International Airport, and desks in the following malls: Deira City Centre, BurJuman Centre, Wafi City, Mercato and Ibn Battuta. The head office is on floors 10–12 of the National Bank of Dubai building on the Deira Creekside.

UK 4th Floor, 41–46 Nuffield House, Piccadilly, London W10DS, tel: 020 7321 6110, e-mail: dtcm_uk@dubaitourism.ae.

North America 25 West 45th Street, Suite #405, New York, NY 10036; tel: +1 212 575 2262; e-mail: dtcm_usa@dubaitourism.ae.

Australia & New Zealand Level 6, 75 Miller Street, North Sydney, NSW 2060; tel: +61 2 9956 6620; e-mail: dtcm_aus@dubaitourism.ae.

South Africa PO Box 698, 1 Orchard Lane, Rivonia 2128, Johannesburg; tel: +27 11 785 4600; e-mail: dtcm_sa@dubaitourism.ae.

TRAVELLERS WITH DISABILITIES

Dubai is one of the Middle East's most accessible destinations. Most of the city's more upmarket hotels now have specially adapted rooms for disabled travellers, and some of the city's malls include disabled parking spaces and specially equipped toilets. Transport is also fairly well adapted. Dubai Taxi (tel: 04 208 0808) has specially designed vehicles equipped with ramps and lifts, while the Metro features tactile guide paths, lifts and ramps to assist visually- and mobility-impaired visitors, as well as wheelchair spaces in all compartments, The city's waterbuses can also be used by mobility-impaired visitors, and staff will assist you in boarding and disembarking, while there are also dedicated facilities for passengers with special needs at the airport. Sadly, but not surprisingly, most of the city's older heritage buildings are not accessible (although the Dubai Museum is an exception).

W

WEBSITES AND INTERNET ACCESS

The following websites are useful sources of information:

www.7days.ae 7Days

www.arabianbusiness.com Arabian Business

www.ameinfo.com AME Info

www.business24-7.ae Emirates Business 24/7

www.dm.gov.ae Dubai Municipality

www.dubaiairport.com Dubai International Airport

www.dubaidutyfree.com Dubai Duty Free

www.dubaitourism.ae Government of Dubai Department of Tourism and Commerce Marketing

www.emirates.com Emirates (airline)

www.gulfnews.com Gulf News

www.princesshaya.net Princess Haya Bint Al Hussein

www.sheikhmohammed.co.ae Sheikh Mohammed Bin Rashid Al Maktoum

www.uaeinteract.com UAE Ministry of Information and Culture

Local telecoms operators Etisalat and Du are the only providers of internet services; note that access to certain websites may be blocked due to political, religious or sexual content. Internet connections are available in the guest rooms and business centres of larger hotels, although often at exorbitant rates. Internet cafés are surprisingly thin on the ground except for in Bur Dubai (where they can be found in many of the small roads and alleyways off Al Fahidi Street). Reliable places are the Al Jalssa internet café (Dhs-10dhr; daily 8am–midnight) in the Al Ain centre and the Grano Coffee shop in Wafi (Dhs14/hr).

The whole of the Dubai Mall is a free WiFi hotspot and you can also get online on the Dubai Metro for Dhs10 per hour. Various WiFi hotspots are operated by Eitsalat (www.etisalat.ae) and Du (www.du.ae). See the websites for full details of charges and hotspot locations.

Recommended Hotels

Accommodation in Dubai doesn't come cheap, but standards at the city's top hotels rival anywhere in the world, offering unparalleled levels of style and luxury. Broadly speaking, hotels divide into beachfront resort-style hotels, almost all of which are located in the southern part of the city, and business-oriented hotels, the best of which can be found strung along or near to Sheikh Zayed Road. There are also a handful of good places in or around the old city centre. There is plenty of cheaper accommodation in the areas around the Creek as well, although standards are more basic.

The accommodation listed below ranges from inexpensive holiday apartments to icons of contemporary opulence like the Burj al Arab (popularly dubbed the world's first 'seven-star' hotel). The price categories indicated by $ symbols next to the hotel name include an additional 20 percent tax and service charge where this is applicable, but if you telephone a hotel yourself, in most cases the figure you'll be quoted won't include this 20 percent. The rate quoted is for room only – breakfast is an additional Dhs75–100.

The price categories below are based on the high-season rate for a standard room for two people. They do not indicate star rating.

$$$$	Dhs3,500–8,000
$$$	Dhs2,500–3,500
$$	Dhs1,000–2,500
$	Under Dhs1,000

DUBAI

THE COAST

Al Qasr $$$$ *Madinat Jumeirah, tel: 04 366 8888, www.jumeirah.com.* Its Arabic name means 'The Palace', and this grand boutique hotel really is fit for a king. Part of the Arabian-style Madinat Jumeirah resort next to Burj al Arab, Al Qasr boasts a palatial gated entrance and opulent interiors, and shares 1km (½ mile) of beach with the resort's other hotel, Mina A'Salam. Its restaurants include the excellent

Pierchic, at the end of a wooden pier jutting into the Gulf from the hotel's gardens. For extra privacy, 29 summer houses, located around a picturesque network of canals, are also available.

Atlantis The Palm $$$ *Palm Jumeirah, tel: 04 426 0000, www.atlantis thepalm.com.* Having opened in style, with a launch party that saw Hollywood's A-listers walk down the red carpet, this popular theme resort houses 1,373 lavish guest rooms and 166 suites – including the Lost Chambers, with their mesmerising underwater views. With a dazzling mix of leisure facilities, retail outlets and eateries like Nobu and Ossiano, Atlantis, The Palm is already an iconic tourist attraction.

Burj Al Arab $$$$ *Umm Suqeim, tel: 04 301 7777, www.jumeirah.com.* A stay in this iconic 'seven-star' hotel offers the last word in opulence, with every mod-con and indulgence you could imagine (and several you probably couldn't), ranging from remote-control curtains to 'pillow menus'. Suites are huge, butlers come as standard and the whole place screams luxury, although at an inevitably stratospheric price – you'll be stretched to find a room for much under $2,000 a night.

Dubai Marine Beach Resort & Spa $$ *Jumeira Road, Jumeira 1, tel: 04 346 1111, www.dxbmarine.com.* Not to be confused with Dubai Marina along the coast, Dubai Marine is the closest beach resort to the city, a short walk across Jumeira Road from Jumeira Mosque. It offers 195 rooms in villa-style low-rise buildings in a landscaped compound fronting on to a small beach. It also has some of the city's best nightspots, including Sho Cho and Boudoir.

Grosvenor House $$ *Dubai Marina, tel: 04 399 8888, www.grosvenor house-dubai.com.* Although it's not located on the beach, this 45-storey Le Meridien property offers stunning views of the coast, including The Palm Jumeirah and Dubai Marina. Guests can use the beach facilities at the nearby Le Royal Meridien Beach Resort. Notable nightspots at the hotel include Bar 44 and Buddha Bar.

Jumeirah Beach Hotel $$$ *Umm Suqeim, tel: 04 348 0000, www. jumeirah.com.* Shaped like a breaking wave to complement nearby Burj al Arab's 'sail', the 26-storey landmark is one of the best beachside hotels in Dubai for both families and couples, with stunning architecture, excellent family facilities, superb grounds and a plethora of restaurants and bars.

Jumeirah Zabeel Saray $$$ *The Palm Jumeirah, tel: 04 453 0000, www.jumeirah.com*. One of the first hotels to open on the outer breakwater of The Palm Jumeirah, this opulent new place has lavish Ottoman styling, with a range of beautifully designed rooms and villas, plus the sumptuous Talisse Ottoman Star and a clutch of excellent eating and drinking venues.

Le Royal Meridien $$$ *Dubai Marina, tel: 04 399 5555, www.leroyal meridien-dubai.com*. This old resort hotel lacks the style of nearby establishments but compensates with superb outdoor facilities – a huge pool, vast gardens and a superb swathe of beach. One of the best places in the city for families.

Mina A'Salam $$ *Madinat Jumeirah, tel: 04 366 8888, www.jumeirah.com*. A shade less expensive than the nearby Al Qasr, the Madinat Jumeirah resort's second grand hotel impresses with its fabulous faux-Arabian architecture and waterfront setting. Meaning 'Port of Peace', Mina A'Salam is connected via canals and walkways to Souk Madinat Jumeirah, with all its cafés, restaurants and bars.

One&Only Royal Mirage $$$ *Al Sufouh Road, Al Sufouh, tel: 04 399 9999, www.oneandonlyresorts.com*. Until Madinat Jumeirah opened in 2004, the Royal Mirage was the only hotel on the coast that could offer an Arabian (or, at least, Moroccan) look and feel, and despite the competition it still takes some beating. Located on 1km (½ mile) of waterfront, the Royal Mirage offers 250 rooms in the Palace, 170 in the Arabian Court and 50 in the exclusive Residence & Spa. The hotel's venues include the excellent Eauzone and Tagine restaurant, Rooftop bar and Kasbar nightclub, plus superb spa.

The Ritz-Carlton Dubai $$$ *Dubai Marina, tel: 04 399 4000, www.ritzcarlton.com*. A little bit of Andalusia in the Gulf, the low-lying hacienda-style Ritz-Carlton has 138 rooms, all sea-facing. More than any other hotel on the coast, it's a quiet retreat for rest and relaxation, far removed from the distractions and crowds of larger beach resorts. In-house amenities include the highly rated French-style La Baie fine-dining restaurant.

SHEIKH ZAYED ROAD

Armani Hotel $$$ *Burj Khalifa, Downtown Dubai; tel: 04 888 3888 http://dubai.armanihotels.com*. Occupying the lower floors of the Burj Khalifa, the world's first Armani hotel offers pretty much the last word in designer minimalism – although prices are less stratospheric than you might expect.

Fairmont Dubai $$$ *Sheikh Zayed Road, tel: 04 332 5555, www.fairmont.com*. Located at the northern end of Sheikh Zayed Road, the Fairmont is one of the most luxurious hotels along the road, with plush rooms, a fancy spa and a pair of fourth-floor pools. The space-age interior boasts the popular Spectrum On One restaurant and Exchange Grills restaurant.

Ibis World Trade Centre $ *Sheikh Zayed Road/Trade Centre 2, tel: 04 332 4444, www.ibishotel.com*. This simple but comfortable four-star is perhaps the best-value hotel in the city, although rooms can get booked up quickly if there is a big event on at the Dubai International Exhibition Centre next door.

Jumeirah Emirates Towers Hotel $$$ *Sheikh Zayed Road, tel: 04 330 0000, www.jumeirah.com*. Part of the Jumeirah Group's portfolio, the landmark 305m (1,000ft) Emirates Towers Hotel has frequently been voted one of the world's best business hotels. Each of the 400 rooms, over 51 floors, has a dedicated workstation with ultra high-speed internet connection, wireless keyboard and fax/printer with private number. Its bars and restaurants include Vu's, the separate Vu's Bar and The Agency.

The Palace – The Old Town $$$ *Emaar Boulevard, The Old Town Island, Downtown Dubai, tel: 04 428 7888, www.theaddress.com*. The Palace is exactly what the name suggests – an opulent hotel reminiscent of an old Arabian palace. Only in this case, the traditional Arabesque facade is complemented with contemporary interiors that are no less luxurious than you would expect in a royal palace. It has views of the Dubai Fountain and the marvellous Burj Khalifa, and is close to Dubai Mall, as well as to the business districts. There are three restaurants, including the excellent Thiptara.

Shangri-La Hotel $$ *Sheikh Zayed Road, tel: 04 343 8888, www. shangri-la.com.* The most appealing hotel on Sheikh Zayed Road, set in a towering, Gotham-esque structure at the southern end of the strip. Inside the hotel is a model of Zen cool, with beautiful rooms (many with outstanding views) and a string of excellent restaurants.

BUR DUBAI

Arabian Courtyard $ *Al Fahidi St, Bur Dubai, tel: 04-351 9111, www.arabiancourtyard.com.* Overlooking the Dubai Museum, this attractive four-star could hardly be more central or better positioned for forays into the old city centre. Inside, there are attractive rooms with Arabian touches and some good eating and drinking spots.

Four Points Sheraton Bur Dubai $ *Khalid Bin Al Waleed Street (Bank Street), tel: 04 397 7444, www.fourpoints.com/burdubai.* Right in the heart of the old city, this comfortable and competitively priced four-star makes an excellent base for exploring Bur Dubai and Deira and boasts good facilities, including the lovely Antique Bazaar restaurant and the cosy Viceroy Pub.

Golden Sands $ *Between Mankhool Road and Sheikh Khalifa Bin Zayed Road (Trade Centre Road), tel: 04 355 5553, www.goldensands dubai.com.* A vast number of pleasant self-catering studios and apartments, scattered over 11 separate buildings in the Al Mankhool area of Bur Dubai – often some of the cheapest lodgings in town, if you don't mind foregoing traditional hotel facilities.

Grand Hyatt Dubai $$ *Sheikh Rashid Road, Umm Hurair, tel: 04 317 1234, www.dubai.grand.hyatt.com.* A rare resort-type hotel in the centre of the city, the 674-room Grand Hyatt lies roughly halfway between the airport and Sheikh Zayed Road. The central location makes the hotel a good base for sightseeing or business meetings on either side of the Creek, though nearby Garhoud Bridge is a traffic bottleneck during the morning and evening rush hour. The hotel is also convenient for Wafi and for zipping along Route 44 towards Al Ain or the Hatta road.

XVA Hotel $ *Bastakiya, tel: 04 353 5383, www.xvahotel.com*. No other paid accommodation in Dubai can compete with the XVA Gallery's authentic Arabian offering. More a guesthouse than a hotel – too small to qualify for a star rating – the XVA is first and foremost an art gallery and coffee shop set around the inner courtyard of a restored home in the city's historic Bastakiya district. Its eight guest rooms, furnished in Arabian style, are on the first-floor rooftop, which offers wonderful views of the Creek skyline and the wind-towers on nearby buildings.

DEIRA

Hilton Dubai Creek $$ *Baniyas Road, tel: 04 227 1111, www.hilton. co.uk/dubaicreek*. Designed by Carlos Ott, the 154-room Hilton Dubai Creek is a stylish, contemporary hotel, set back on the land side of Baniyas Road, with outstanding views of the nearby dhow wharves, as well as of the distant Sheikh Zayed Road skyline, from its Creek-facing rooms.

Hyatt Regency Dubai $$ *Corniche Road, tel: 04 209 1234, www. dubai.regency.hyatt.com*. A distinctive dark monolith overlooking the mouth of Dubai Creek, this is one of the city's oldest five-stars, although refurbishments have kept things fresh. All rooms have sea views, while popular in-house restaurants include the Mediterranean Focaccia and the Japanese Miyako. The hotel also has Dubai's only revolving restaurant, the rooftop Al Dawaar.

Park Hyatt $$$ *Dubai Creek Golf & Yacht Club, tel: 04 602 1234, www.dubai.park.hyatt.com*. Rivalling the nearby Raffles for the title of the city centre's top place to stay, this idyllic city retreat occupies a sprawl of Moroccan-style buildings spread along the Creek between the Dubai Creek and Golf clubs, with gorgeous Arabian styling and superb views.

Radisson Blu $ *Baniyas Road, tel: 04 222 7171, www.deiracreek.dubai. radissonsas.com*. The first chain hotel in Dubai when it opened as the InterContinental in 1975, the 276-room Radisson Blu remains a firm favourite, thanks to its central location overlooking the creek. Among the hotel's venues are the hip Italian restaurant La Moda and Up On The 10th, one of the best live jazz venues in town. The dhow wharves are within walking distance and the Deira souks are a short cab ride away.

Raffles $$$ *Sheikh Rashid Rd, Wafi, tel: 04-324 8888, www.raffles.com*. Spectacular hotel housed in a giant pyramid, with a mix of quirky Egyptian theming and cool Asian designs, plus superb facilities including huge gardens, a gorgeous spa and some excellent restaurants and bars.

OUTSIDE THE CITY

Al Maha Desert Resort & Spa $$$$ *Interchange No. 8, Dubai–Al Ain Road, tel: 04 832 9900, www.al-maha.com*. The Al Maha eco-resort, 40km (25 miles) from Dubai, is a world-class destination with prices to match. Resembling a luxury tented camp within the 225 sq km (87 sq mile) Dubai Desert Conservation Reserve, the 'six-star' resort is named after the Arabian oryx *(al maha)* that live and breed in the surrounding dunes. Each of its 40 suites has a private pool. Horse riding, camel trekking and falconry are among the activities for guests, plus an alluring spa.

Bab al Shams Desert Resort & Spa $$ *Endurance City, tel: 04 809 6100, www.meydanhotels.com/babalshams*. If the budget won't stretch to Al Maha, consider Bab al Shams (literally 'Gate of the Sun'), in a desert fort setting among the dunes near Dubai's centre for endurance riding, 37km (23 miles) from Dubai Autodrome.

Hatta Fort Hotel $ *Hatta, tel: 04 852 3211, www.jebelali-international. com*. Before the Al Maha resort and Bab al Shams, the four-star Hatta Fort Hotel was the only retreat from the city that promised a bit of luxury. Set among the mountains of the Hajar range, near the border with Oman, an hour's drive from Dubai, the Hatta Fort may be a little dated now, but its appeal is enduring. Its 50 chalets have views of the mountains, which can be explored on 4x4 trips arranged by the hotel.

INDEX

Berlitz pocket guide

Dubai

Third Edition 2012

Written by Matt Jones
Updated by Gavin Thomas
Edited by Scarlett O'Hara and Siân Lezard
Picture Researcher: Lucy Johnston
Series Editor: Tom Stainer
Production: Tynan Dean, Linton Donaldson and Rebeka Ellam

Photography credits: Chris Bradley 81, 83; Corbis 24, 52, 89, 91, 104; Kevin Cummins/APA 4TL, 4BL, 4BC, 4-5B, 12, 43, 55, 61, 87, 92; Dubai Tourism 3CR, 3BR, 5BC, 5BR, 69, 70, 92, 100; Fotolia 1, 2BL, 10; iStockphoto 2TR, 2BR, 3TL, 3CL, 4TR, 5TL, 5TR, 8, 14, 26, 34, 35, 36, 37, 39, 40, 46, 49, 54, 58, 60, 65, 66, 71, 72, 74, 82, 84, 97, 102, 103, 106, 109; Matt Jones 3BL, 16, 18, 20, 29, 30, 32, 41, 44, 47, 50, 57, 63, 76, 79, 98; Topham 22.

Cover picture: 4Corners Images

Every effort has been made to provide accurate information in this publication, but changes are inevitable. The publisher cannot be responsible for any resulting loss, inconvenience or injury.

Contact us

At Berlitz we strive to keep our guides as accurate and up to date as possible, but if you find anything that has changed, or if you have any suggestions on ways to improve this guide, then we would be delighted to hear from you.

Berlitz Publishing, PO Box 7910, London SE1 1WE, England.
email: berlitz@apaguide.co.uk
www.berlitzpublishing.com

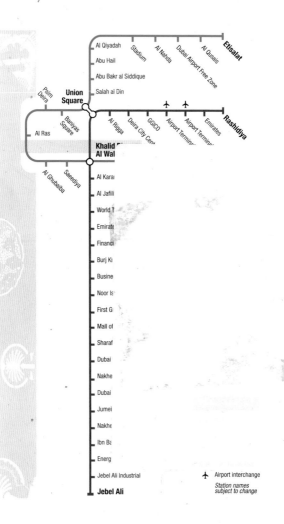

Al Qiyadah

Abu Hail

Abu Bakr al Siddique

Salah al Din

Union Square

Palm Deira

Banyas Square

Al Ras

Stadium

Al Nahda

Dubai Airport Free Zone

Al Qusais

Etisalat

Al Rigga

Deira City Cent...

GGICO

Airport Termin...

Airport Termin...

Emirates

Rashidiya

Khalid B...
Al Wal...

Al Ghubaiba

Saeediya

Al Kara...

Al Jafili...

World T...

Emirate...

Financi...

Burj K...

Busine...

Noor Is...

First G...

Mall of...

Sharaf...

Dubai...

Nakhe...

Dubai...

Jumei...

Nakhe...

Ibn Ba...

Energ...

Jebel Ali Industrial

Jebel Ali

✈ Airport interchange

Station names
subject to change